Contents

Unit	Topics	Functions
1	**Moving on to New Experiences** Moving on to another class and a new teacher; goodbyes; remembering good times; life decisions; daily routine; comparing cultures; lifestyles; comparing education systems	Talking about things that happened in the past; ending a conversation appropriately; talking about future plans; expressing obligation; indicating necessity; expressing hope; discussing cross-cultural experiences; comparing and contrasting lifestyles across cultures; asking for an opinion; giving an opinion
2	**Meeting New Friends and Acquaintances** Meeting new classmates; beginning classes in a new program/in a new country; getting acquainted; appropriate classroom behavior; cultural differences	Exchanging information about personal history; talking about oneself and one's experiences; expressing understanding or lack of understanding; clarifying information; introducing oneself and others in a group; asking and talking about class rules and regulations; describing appropriate classroom behavior; discussing cultural adaptation; expressing conclusions
3	**Changing Times** The Generation Gap; four different generations in the U.S.; "the good old days;" changing times; contributions of senior citizens; traditionally male/female roles; personal goals; Nelson Mandela; goals/heros	Confirming information; talking about the past; expressing one's opinions; expressing goals; writing a letter defending one's opinion; identifying the main idea; reading for specific information; arranging events in chronological order; writing a definition of a hero
4	**Illness and Health** Illness and treatment; schedules; journals; emergency care; a hospital bill; warnings on medicine labels; health insurance	Describing a sequence of events in the past; writing a journal entry; asking for and giving reasons; discussing a visit to an emergency room; reporting direct speech; understanding a hospital bill; demonstrating understanding of medicine labels; discussing health insurance and how it works; scanning for specific information; discussing the relationship between lifestyle and health
5	**Change for the Better** Culture shock and reverse culture shock; young people in the United States; the suburbs and the city; likes and dislikes	Discussing cross-cultural experiences; talking about ongoing experiences; making inferences; asking for and giving an opinion; using time expressions; stating one's opinion about information from a survey; reading for specific information; expressing observations about the surroundings and the environment; giving an opinion about an issue; asking for and giving a reason
6	**Love and Marriage** Relationships and marriage; personal ads; emotions; matchmaking; marriage customs; stages of marriage	Discussing relationships and marriage; expressing agreement and disagreement; giving reasons; describing emotions; comparing dating and marriage customs in different countries; expressing preferences; talking about feelings and emotions; expressing similarities and differences; expressing results
7	**The Job Marketplace** Part-time jobs related to future careers; job duties and responsibilities; work environment preferences; comparing wages; evaluating jobs	Giving advice; expressing obligation; discussing job searches; making suggestions; identifying personal skills and abilities; interpreting a bar graph; interpreting information on a pay stub; discussing advantages and disadvantages of job
8	**Road Safety** Road test for a driver's license; traffic safety; traffic signs; accident prevention; transportation expenses	Interpreting driving regulations; identifying traffic signs; giving advice about road safety; describing an accident to the police; calling for road assistance; filling in information on a form; expressing and accepting apologies; reading and interpreting information in a bar graph; giving advice; giving one's opinions; comparing solutions
9	**Confronting Everyday Realities** Keeping a budget; saving money; lifestyle choices; goals for the future; advertisements	Describing problems and their solutions; making suggestions; calculating percentages; filling in missing information on a billing statement; offering solutions and suggestions; drawing conclusions; describing feelings; reading and understanding the fine print in ads; comparing products; making polite requests
10	**Following a Dream** Sports and recreation; vacations; personal experiences; plans for the future	Discussing recreational activities; offering suggestions and advice; expressing enthusiasm; expressing fatigue; brainstorming possible solutions to a problem; talking about vacation plans; talking about possibilities; talking about past opportunities; talking about past abilities; giving an excuse; talking about learning from past experiences; writing and talking about future plans; writing and delivering a speech

Grammmar and Pronunciation	Listening and Speaking	Reading and Writing
• Simple past: regular/irregular verbs • Past continuous and simple past • Future tense, *will* and *be going to* • Necessity: *must, don't have to* • *Hope* + future clauses • Additions with *too, not either,* and *but* • Contractions with *will*	Listen for details; describe a recent experience; listen and take notes; end a conversation appropriately; discuss making important decisions; put tasks in logical order; discuss schedules; express opinions; interview a partner and take notes	Read an article for details; guess meaning from context; write a note; fill in a questionnaire; set up a personal journal
• Modals: *can, may, should, ought to, must, must not* • Present perfect with *since, for* • Stress in questions and answers with *can/can't*	Listen to a conversation for details; listen, take notes, and compare information; give instructions; express understanding or lack of understanding; describe an embarrassing situation; make introductions; express agreement or disagreement; listen to/role play a request for assistance in a problem situation	Write a paragraph describing a good English teacher; write a dialogue for a role-play; make inferences and draw conclusions about pictures; make and post a list of helpful classroom behaviors
• Present perfect tag questions • *used to* • Comparison of adjectives and adverbs • *Wh-* questions • Tag questions: rising–falling *vs.* rising intonation)	Check for confirmation; elicit agreeing and disagreeing responses by asking tag questions; ask for and give opinions; listen for chronological order; discuss a word definition	Read for specific information; determine the meaning of new vocabulary from context; identify main ideas; make inferences; write an opinion letter; write a definition; write a biographical paragraph
• Complex sentences with time clauses • Cause/effect • Direct speech • Comparisons with *as/not as*	Ask for and give reasons for certain procedures; interview a classmate; report the actual words someone said; listen for specific details in a phone call; make recommendations	Understand charges on a bill; understand medicine labels; scan for specific information; write a journal entry; make a list of recommendations
• Present perfect continuous; affirmative, interrogative, and negative • Passive voice; affirmative and interrogative • Sense/Perception Verbs + Adjective • Present continuous vs. Simple present • Sentence stress and rhythm	Discuss the meaning of new terms; listen to details and make conclusions; give an oral presentation in class; express opinions based on a written text; state advantages and disadvantages; give reasons for likes and dislikes; conduct an opinion survey	Read for specific information; make inferences; support opinions with examples from a written text; write a journal entry
• State verbs • Adjective/Noun • Prepositional phrase: *because of;* complex sentence: *because* • *Would rather, would prefer* • Compound sentences with *and, but* and *so* •Contractions with *would rather*	Listen and express opinions based on the listening; compare marriage customs; express preferences	Read the personals; write a personal ad; read for details; make inferences; paraphrase information; make conclusions based on specific details
• Unreal conditions in the present/future • Modals: *be supposed to* (questions and statements) • *Too/ very/ enough* • Verb + gerund • Contractions with *would*	Listen and express opinions based on the listening; respond to difficult situations; listen for specific details and make inferences; give advice	Understand words from context; read and write an ad; make inferences; interpret a bar graph; read for main ideas and supporting details; interpret information on a pay stub; prioritize a list
• *Had better* • Gerund as subject • Gerund after preposition • Questions with *How* • *It is* + adjective + infinitive • Syllable shift	Listen for details; give advice; describe a personal experience; listen and role-play a similar situation	Interpret driving regulations; identify traffic signs; fill in information on a form; read and make conclusions; interpret information from a bar graph; read and infer the main idea
• *If* clauses with modals • Participial adjectives • Verb + infinitive • Comparison of nouns • Modals: requests • Intonation	Describe problems and their solutions; offer solutions and suggestions; discuss the meaning of new expressions; listen for specific details (numbers) and draw conclusions; compare products; make polite requests; role play a situation	Calculate percentages and charges; read ads and understand the fine print; write a television ad
• Real conditions in the present • Modals: *may/might; was/were able to/could* • Gerund as subject • Complex clauses • *-ing* (pronunciation)	Listen for details; role play a problem situation; brainstorm possible solutions to a problem; talk about possibilities; role play giving an excuse; talk about future plans; deliver a speech	Brainstorm meanings of unfamiliar vocabulary/determine meanings in picture contexts; read travel ads for specific details; write short dialogs; write about future plans; write a speech

To the Teacher

New Vistas is a series that features the best of what has come to be known as "communicative language teaching," including recent developments in creating interactive, learner-centered curriculum. With *New Vistas,* your students become actively involved in their own language acquisition through collaboration with you as their guide and facilitator.

The Components of *New Vistas*

Student Books

The five-level student books begin with *Getting Started.* Here, students learn basic life skills and vocabulary. Then, in the subsequent levels, students develop their competence and proficiency step by step in all four skills.

Primary features of all the *Student Books* include a storyline with multi-ethnic characters, providing students with opportunities to be personally involved in real-life contexts for learning; a carefully graded series of pronunciation modules; many opportunities for group and pair interaction; listening comprehension exercises; a new and exciting online feature that introduces students to Internet technology; a strategy-awareness section in each unit that stimulates students to reflect on their own preferred pathways to success; and end-of-unit grammar and communication skills summaries.

Teacher's Resource Manuals

For each unit, the *Teacher's Resource Manual* provides an overview of topics, functions, communication skills, and skills standards covered. This is followed by step-by-step, explicit teaching instructions; answer keys for the exercises in the *Student Books* and the *Workbooks,* tapescripts for the listening and pronunciation exercises; grammar activity masters; and placement and achievement tests.

Workbooks

These supplements provide numerous written exercises that reinforce the grammar points and structures taught in the *Student Books. Workbook* exercises are suitable for additional in-class practice or for homework.

The Audio Programs

The audiotapes provide stimulating listening and pronunciation practice that add to the authenticity of classroom pedagogy.

UNIT 1

Lesson 1

In this lesson, you will
- talk about things that happened in the past.
- end a conversation appropriately.

Let's keep in touch!

Listen and read.

Oscar: Are you ready to start classes?

Nelson: I guess so, but I'm going to miss Mrs. Brennan. I'm sorry that she's leaving.

Oscar: Yeah, me too. Mrs. Brennan's class was a lot of fun.

Nelson: Yes, it was. We had a lot of good times together and we learned a lot.

Oscar: Especially when you fell asleep in class!

Nelson: I remember that—when I fell asleep while everyone was taking the midterm exam.

Oscar: You were very tired, I guess.

Nelson: Yes, I was. The night before the exam I stayed up very late. While I was trying to study for the midterm, Tony was watching an exciting soccer game. We went to bed at 2 A.M.

Yumiko: I almost cried when class ended yesterday.

Mrs. Brennan: I understand. But we're not saying good-bye. We'll always remain friends.

Yumiko: Yes, I know. But we'll still miss you, Mrs. Brennan. Let's keep in touch!

(Vamos a mantenernos in contacto)

<u>Pair</u> Who is your best friend? How did you meet this person? Why is this friendship important to you?

① remain [rɪ'meɪn] (be left over) sobrar, restar (survive) quedar;
remained   (stay, persist) quedarse
it will remain in my memory = seme quedara grabado en la memoria

UNIT 1   **1**

1 What happened last semester?

Pair Complete the sentences about the students in Mrs. Brennan's class. Use the simple past tense verbs in the box below.

Regular Past Tense	Irregular Past Tense
work → worked study → studied (note spelling change)	fall → fell, sleep → slept, feel → felt, eat → ate buy → bought, make → made, give → gave, sit → sat

1. **What happened to Nelson?**

A few days ago, Nelson _studied_ until very late.

The next morning, he _fell_ asleep during the exam.

2. **What happened to Lynn?**

Lynn _ate_ a hamburger at the festival last month.

Later, she _felt_ sick.

3. **What happened to Yumiko?**

Six months ago, Yumiko _sat_ in the back of the class by herself.

A week ago, she _made_ a presentation in front of the class.

Pair Practice asking your partner questions about the pictures above.

Example:

> A: What happened to Nelson during the exam?
> B: He fell asleep.

Tell your partner about something that happened to you recently. Where were you? Who were you with? What happened? How did you feel? What did you learn from the experience?

2 What were you doing at 7 o'clock last night?

Lynn and Yumiko were cooking dinner at 7 o'clock last night. What about their friends? Listen and match the two parts of the sentences.

_____ 1. Ivan   a. was listening to his new CD.

_____ 2. Yon Mi   b. were watching a soccer game at home.

_____ 3. Gina   c. was writing a letter to her fiancé.

_____ 4. Tony and Nelson   d. was reading a book about Italian history.

_____ 5. Oscar   e. was studying in the library.

3 Where were you at 7 o'clock last night?

Pair   Listen to the cassette again. Complete the notes on the index cards below. Then make sentences telling where two people were and what they were doing at the same time.

Name	Place	Activity
Gina		reading a book about Italian history
Nelson	home	
Oscar	home	
Ivan		studying

Name	Place	Activity
Tony		watching the soccer game
Yon Mi	library	

> Ivan **was studying** at the library **while** Tony **was watching** a soccer game at home.
> **While** Tony **was watching** a soccer game at home, Ivan **was studying** at the library.

4 What were you doing when it started to rain?

Read Yon Mi's letter to her fiance, Han. Complete the sentences with the correct form of the verb.

> Lynn **was visiting** Yon Mi when it started to rain.
> **When** Yon Mi **was writing** a letter to Han, she felt happy.

run } correr
ran }
run

trip = viaje
= tropezar
fall } caer
fell }
fallen }
get up = levantarse

Dear Han,

On Saturday Lynn and Gina were visiting me when it began to rain. When we
___ran___ to the house, I ___tripped___ and ___fell___. When I ___got up___, my ankle
    1. run   2. trip   3. fall   4. get up
___hurt___. While Lynn and Gina ___helped___ me into the house, the phone ___rang___.
  5. hurt   6. help   7. ring
When I ___picked up___ the phone, Yumiko ___cried___. She ___worked___ at the bank and
      8. pick up   9. cry   10. work
someone just ___robbed___ the bank.
          12. rob

                               Love,

                               Yon Mi

5 Word Bag: Ending a Conversation

Pair   Ending a conversation can be difficult. Read the following conversation with your partner. Then choose an appropriate ending for each situation below. Use more than one expression, if you wish.

Pablo: It's been a great party, Mrs. Brennan.

Mrs. Brennan: You're not leaving so soon, are you?

Pablo: *Yes, I'm afraid I must be going. I'll see you again soon.*

Informal	More Formal
I have to take off. I've got to get back to work. Let's get together again soon. Thanks for your help.	Thanks for your time. It's been a pleasure to meet you. I'm afraid I must be going. I'll see you again soon. It was good to see you.

1.

The manager of a company is interviewing an applicant for a position in sales.

Manager: Thank you, I don't have any more questions.

Applicant: _____

2.

A guest at a dinner party is very sleepy and wants to go home.

Hostess: I'm going to make some coffee. Can you stay?

Guest: Sorry, I can't. _____

3.

You are studying in the cafeteria when a classmate comes and sits down next to you. You talk for a few minutes, but you want to get back to work.

You: I'd like to talk, but I can't. _____

4.

A nephew is visiting his aunt in the hospital. The visiting hours are almost over.

Aunt: It was so nice of you to visit me. I really appreciate it.

Nephew: _____

Pair   What would you say in the following situations?

• Your cousin has just helped you buy a car. You are leaving him and going home.

• You and your boss are doing some work together. You notice that it's 5 o'clock. You have to leave to pick up your son.

• A taxi-driver has helped you with your luggage. You're getting out of the cab.

• Make up a situation of your own.

In this lesson, you will
- talk about future plans.
- express hope.
- express obligation.
- indicate necessity.

I have something to tell you!

🔊 **Listen and read the following conversation.**

Mrs. Brennan: You've been awfully quiet this evening, Yon Mi. How do you like the party? Are you having fun?

Yon Mi: Yes, I am. It's a wonderful party. Mrs. Brennan, may I ask you a personal question?

Mrs. Brennan: Sure!

Yon Mi: Were you 100 percent sure when you married Mr. Brennan?

Mrs. Brennan: Oh, I don't think anybody can be 100 percent sure, but I was pretty sure. Why?

Yon Mi: Well, do you remember my fiancé, Han? I've decided to go back to Korea and marry him, but I haven't told anybody yet.

Mrs. Brennan: Really? You must tell your friends. Do you want to tell them now?

Yon Mi: Sure.

Mrs. Brennan: Listen everybody! Yon Mi has an announcement to make.

Yon Mi: I want to share something with you. I have to go back to Korea soon. I'm sure you remember Han, my fiancé. Well, we're going to get married in a couple of months.

Mrs. Brennan: I hope you'll have a wonderful life together.

Gina: We're going to miss you very much, Yon Mi.

Yon Mi: I'm going to miss you all too.

Oscar: I hope you will come back and see us again. Maybe for your honeymoon?

Yon Mi: I hope so too.

Pair Do you think Yon Mi made the right decision? Why? What's the most important decision you ever had to make? Tell your partner about it.

1 Yon Mi is getting ready to leave.

Pair Help Yon Mi plan what she has to do before she leaves for Korea on September 30.

return books to the library
buy a plane ticket
pack her suitcases
move out of her apartment

buy gifts for her family and friends
sell her furniture
close her bank accounts and call credit
    card companies
go to a farewell party

SEPTEMBER						
SUNDAY	MONDAY	TUESDAY	WEDNESDAY	THURSDAY	FRIDAY	SATURDAY
17	18 Buy a plane ticket	19	20	21	22	23
24	25	26	27	28	29	30 Fly to Seoul

Ask your partner questions about Yon Mi's plans for next week.

Example:

When is Yon Mi going to buy a plane ticket?

She's going to buy the plane ticket on Monday, September 18.

2 I'll get the traveler's checks.

Mr. and Mrs. Brennan are also leaving the country—to work in the Middle East for three years. Listen to their conversation and write what each one will do in the next few days.

> Mrs. Brennan will pick up the plane tickets.
>
> Mr. Brennan will get the traveler's checks.

Mrs. Brennan

1. _____
2. _____
3. _____
4. _____
5. _____

Mr. Brennan

1. _____
2. _____
3. _____
4. _____
5. _____

Pair Discuss your plans for next week or next weekend. Then report your partner's plans to the class.

3 You must take off your shoes!

Group Some friends from another country are planning a trip to your country. You invite them to your house for dinner. Tell them about the cultural and social rules to prepare them for the visit. Use *have to, must, don't have to,* and *must not.*

> You **must take off** your shoes before you enter a house.
>
> You **must not take off** your shoes before you enter a house.
>
> You **don't have to take off** your shoes before you enter a house.

1. Take off your shoes.

2. Bring a present (or flowers).

3. Shake hands.

4. Kiss your host on both cheeks.

5. Finish the food on your plate.

6. Stand up when an elderly person comes into the room.

4 Hear it. Say it.

Listen to the following sentences.

Contractions with *will*

1. I'll make many friends.
2. You'll like the class.
3. She'll pass the TOEFL®.
4. He'll find a job.
5. They'll have a chance to practice English.
6. We'll have time to do our homework.
7. She'll have a happy life with Han.
8. It'll be a nice surprise.

Pair Take turns pronouncing the sentences.

5 I hope I'll make many friends.

Pair Look at the list below. Check (✔) the things that you hope you will do and put an X next to the things you hope you won't do during the semester.

Then make a sentence with *I hope* and a future verb for each item.

> *I hope* I'll *make* a lot of friends.
>
> *I hope* I *won't* fail the class.

_____ 1. make a lot of friends

_____ 2. like the class

_____ 3. waste my time

_____ 4. have time to do all my homework

_____ 5. pass the TOEFL®

_____ 6. fail the class

_____ 7. have a chance to practice my English

_____ 8. find a job

Now add two more examples of your own.

6 I hope you'll be lucky together.

Pair Some of Yon Mi's classmates have signed a farewell card for her. Read their card and write three farewell sentences with *hope*.

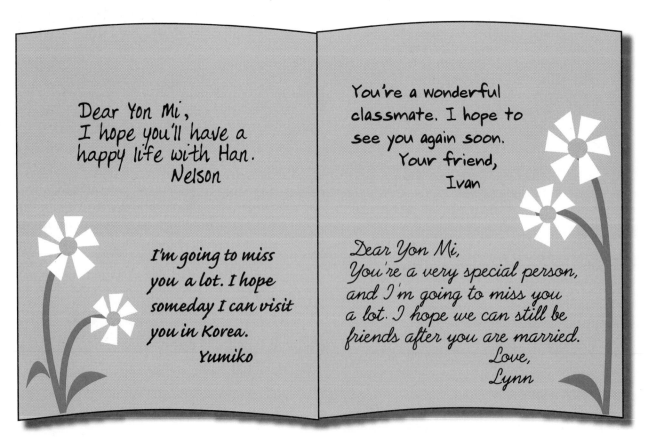

Dear Yon Mi,
I hope you'll have a
happy life with Han.
        Nelson

I'm going to miss
you a lot. I hope
someday I can visit
you in Korea.
        Yumiko

You're a wonderful
classmate. I hope to
see you again soon.
        Your friend,
        Ivan

Dear Yon Mi,
You're a very special person,
and I'm going to miss you
a lot. I hope we can still be
friends after you are married.
        Love,
        Lynn

Lesson 3

In this lesson, you will

- discuss cross-cultural experiences.
- compare and contrast lifestyles across cultures.
- ask for an opinion.
- give an opinion.

The Colorful Years

Listen and read the article.

ESL students at Abraham Lincoln High School in San Francisco have the best of both worlds. "They participate in a wide variety of activities that make their high school life colorful," says Fan Fang, director of the Chinese Two-Way Immersion Program. "Our Chinese Cyber Academic Center reflects an international effort to establish a resource center and study hall in Chinese on the Internet. Students use Chinese to communicate with other Internet users in China, Hong Kong, Taiwan, and the United Kingdom. They have Chinese e-mail pen pals around the world now."

"Our Chinese Two-Way Immersion Program," Fang continues, "provides ESL students with the opportunity to improve their English by interacting with native speakers both in language development classes and in content areas."

Lincoln High School ESL students also participate in the editing and publishing of the student online Chinese magazine, *The Colorful Years*, with other middle and high school students in San Francisco, Taiwan, Hong Kong and Manila.

Each issue of *The Colorful Years* features school news, student cultural news, current events that students are interested in, psychological tests, popular polls, puzzles, and more. The magazine builds a bridge for students around the world to discuss academic problems and assignments in Chinese.

"Lincoln's program is distinctive because it is technology-based," comments Fang. "Students receive technology assistance in their language learning and learn the most advanced computer applications in processing Chinese at the same time. The technology enrichment of our language programs will surely prepare our students to be the next century's active global-village participants."

2

Source: Published by permission of Fan Fang, Director of the Chinese Two-Way Immersion Program, Abraham Lincoln High School, San Francisco, CA. (colorful_years @ hotmail.com)

Pair   **What kind of language learner are you? What do you think is the best way to learn another language?**

1 He gets up at 6 o'clock and goes to school at 7 o'clock.

Pair   Look at a typical day in the life of Martin Yu, a Chinese high school student in San Francisco. Take turns asking and answering questions about his daily life. Partner A, cover the Weekday Schedule. Partner B, cover the Weekend Schedule.

A: **What time does** Martin get up?

B: He **gets up** at 6:00.

A: **Does** he **eat** breakfast at 7:00?

B: No, he **doesn't**. He **goes** to school then.

WEEKDAYS		WEEKENDS	
6:00 **get up**	6:00 **review lessons**	8:00 **get up**	2:00 **go shopping**
6:30 **eat breakfast**	7:00 **have dinner**	8:30 **eat breakfast**	4:00 **study**
7:00 **go to school**	8:00 **do homework**	9:00 **go to swimming class**	6:00 **have dinner**
7:30 **attend classes**	10:00 **watch TV**	12:00 **return home**	7:00 **go out with friends**
5:30 **return home**	11:00 **go to bed**	12:30 **have lunch**	12:00 **go to bed**

2 Martin gets up at 6, and I do too.

Weekdays	Weekends
Martin **gets up** at 6, and I **do too**.	Martin **doesn't get up** at 9, and I **don't either**.
I go to school at 7, and Martin **does too**.	I **don't get** up at 9, and Martin **doesn't either**.
Martin **reviews** his lessons, but I **don't**.	I **don't attend swimming classes**, but Martin **does**.

Pair   Fill in the chart of your daily activities for a weekday and a weekend. Show it to your partner. Compare your daily activities and lifestyles. Are they similar or different?

Weekdays		Weekends	

Now compare your schedules with Martin's. What similarities or differences do you find in the schedules? Compare your lifestyle with Martin's. Describe the similarities and differences.

3 High school enrollment is compulsory.

🎧 Listen to the following description of educational systems in Taiwan and the United States. Then read the statements below and check (✔) the country each statement refers to.

		Taiwan	United States
1.	Most of the people are able to read and write.		
2.	Students eat lunch in the school lunchroom.		
3.	Children attend school on Saturday mornings, as well as Monday through Friday.		
4.	Elementary and middle school students usually attend neighborhood schools.		
5.	High school enrollment is compulsory.		
6.	Tests determine what high school students will attend.		

Pair Discuss with your partner the statements above that describe the educational system in your country.

4 My partner doesn't study in the library, and I don't either.

Fill out the following questionnaire about your lifestyle and daily activities.

LIFESTYLE QUESTIONNAIRE

Study Habits   YES   NO
1. Do you study immediately after class? ☐ ☐
2. Do you use a dictionary to look up new words? ☐ ☐
3. Do you study in the library? ☐ ☐
4. Do you memorize grammar rules? ☐ ☐
5. Do you write down the meaning of new words? ☐ ☐

Leisure Activities
1. Do you have a hobby? ☐ ☐
2. Do you play a sport? ☐ ☐
3. Do you play a musical instrument? ☐ ☐
4. Do you like eating out? ☐ ☐
5. Do you go camping or hiking? ☐ ☐

Shopping
1. Do you like shopping for clothes? ☐ ☐
2. Do you like shopping for food? ☐ ☐
3. Do you shop in a supermarket? ☐ ☐
4. Do you shop in an outdoor market? ☐ ☐
5. Do you pay cash for the things you buy? ☐ ☐

Pair Now compare your answers with a partner. Then report your comparisons to the class using *and . . . too, and . . . not either,* or *but.*

Example:
My partner studies in the library, and I do too. She plays tennis, but I don't.

5 Online

Log onto **http://www.prenhall.com/brown_activities**
The Web: Cultural *do's* and *don't's*
Grammar: What's your grammar IQ?
E-mail: Tell me your plans!

6 Wrap Up

Group **Read the college requirements for two countries and discuss the questions.**

COUNTRY Y

Students have to take a national examination to enter any university. They have to be in the top 10 percent of all the students in the country. However, once they are accepted, their education is free or costs very little.

COUNTRY Z

Students can choose from government-supported or private universities, so there are more opportunities to enter a university. However, education is very expensive. Students have to pass certain tests, but they don't have to rank in the top percent of the whole country.

---

1. What are the advantages and disadvantages of each system? Which do you prefer?

2. Should a university education be open to:
   - only students with the best grades?
   - both men and women?
   - international students?
   - older students returning to school?
   - people whose first language is different from the first language of the university?
   - everyone who wants to attend?

3. Do you think it's fair to select students on the basis of a single test? Why or why not? What other criteria can be used? Share your discussion with the class.

Strategies for Success

➤ **Practicing a grammar point meaningfully**
➤ **Linking culture and language**
➤ **Setting personal goals**

1. Tell your Learning Partner what you did (past tense) over the break or vacation just before this course. Try to use as many different verbs as possible.

2. With your partner, talk about differences between your own culture and some other culture. Tell your partner what you like and don't like about both cultures.

3. Set up your journal for the course, and in your first entry, write down at least five major goals that you will try to accomplish during this course. (For example, "I will speak up more in class." "I will practice using the new vocabulary words from each unit in this book." "I will write in my journal at least once a week." "I will create opportunities to listen to English on TV every day." "I will read something in English for 15 minutes every day.")

CHECKPOINT

How much have you learned in this unit? Review the goals for each lesson. What skills can you confidently use now? What skills do you need to practice? List these below.

Skills I've Learned Well

_____

_____

_____

_____

Skills I Need to Practice

_____

_____

_____

_____

Learning Preferences

In this unit, which type of activity did you like the best and the least? Write the number in the box: 1 = best; 2 = next best; 3 = next; 4 = least.

- ☐ Working by myself
- ☐ Working with a partner
- ☐ Working with a group
- ☐ Working as a whole class

In this unit, which exercises helped you to learn to:

listen more effectively? Exercise ____

speak more fluently? Exercise ____

read more easily? Exercise ____

write more clearly? Exercise ____

Which exercise did you like the most? ____ Why? _____

Which exercise did you like the least? ____ Why? _____

VOCABULARY

Miscellaneous
close
compulsory
easily
enrollment
farewell
honeymoon
semester

Regular Verbs
fail
pass
waste (time)

Irregular Verbs
buy-bought-bought
eat-ate-eaten
fall-fell-fallen
feel-felt-felt
give-gave-given
make-made-made
sit-sat-sat
sleep-slept-slept

To end a conversation
I have to take off.
I've got to get back to work.
Let's get together again soon.
Thanks.
Thanks for your time.
It's been a pleasure to meet you.
I'm afraid I must be going.
It was good to see you.
I'll see you again soon.

▶ GRAMMAR SUMMARY

Regular past tense verbs	Irregular past tense verbs
work–worked	fall–fell, sleep–slept, feel–felt, eat–ate,
study–studied (note spelling change)	buy–bought, make–made, give–gave, sit–sat

Past Continuous and Simple Past

I **got** interested in English **while I was going** to high school in my country.
When I **was sightseeing** in New York, **I met** an actress.

Future Tense

Future with *Will*	Future with *Be going to*
She**'ll pick the plane tickets up** on Friday.	She**'s going to buy** the plane tickets on Friday.

Necessity

You **must take off** your shoes before you enter a room. You **don't have to** take off your shoes before you enter a room.

Hope + future clauses

I hope I'll make many friends. I hope I won't fail the class.

Additions with *too, not either,* and *but.*

She **gets up** at 6, and I **do too**. I **go** to school at 6:50, and she **does too**. She **reviews** her school work, but I **don't**.	She **doesn't get up** at 9, and I **don't either**. I **don't get** up at 9, and she **doesn't either**. I **don't review** my school work, but she **does**.

▶ COMMUNICATION SUMMARY

Talking about the past
I got interested in English while I was going to high school in my country.

Ending a conversation appropriately
Let's get together again soon.
It's been a pleasure to meet you.

Talking about future plans
She's going to buy a plane ticket.
He'll get the traveler's checks.

Expressing necessity
You must take off your shoes.
You don't have to bring a present.

Expressing hope
I hope you'll come back and see us again.

Discussing cross-cultural experiences
In the United States, high school enrollment is compulsory.

Comparing and contrasting lifestyles across cultures
Martin has classes on Saturday, but I don't.
He goes to bed late, and I do too.

Asking for an opinion
Do you think a university education should be free?

Giving an opinion
I think a university education should be available for everyone.

UNIT 2

Lesson 1

In this lesson, you will

- exchange information about personal history.
- talk about yourself and your experiences.
- express understanding or lack of understanding.

Let's get to know each other.

🎧 **Listen and read the following conversation.**

Tony: Excuse me, you look familiar. Have I seen you some place before?

Jacques: I think I saw you at the registration for ESL classes.

Tony: Oh, yeah. Is this your first semester?

Jacques: Uh-huh, how did you know?

Tony: I've taken several classes at the World Language Center, and I've never seen you before.

Jacques: I've only been here for a few days. So . . . you must like the program, huh?

Tony: Sure, I've been taking classes here for over a year now, and I think my English has improved a lot in that time. What level are you in?

Jacques: I don't know. I'm taking the placement test tomorrow. I'll find out which class I'm in after that. By the way, my name is Jacques, and this is Sofia. We met at registration. She's new here too.

Tony: It's nice to meet you, Sofia.

Sofia: It's nice to meet you too. Can you tell us about the program? Is it hard?

Tony: Not bad. I've liked all my teachers so far, and I've had lots of opportunities to practice. Hey, do you have time to get a cup of coffee? I can tell you all about it.

Pair   **Is it easy to talk to strangers in your city? Have you ever met someone on a bus or in a park? How did the conversation start?**

1 Haven't I seen you somewhere before?

🎧 Tony thinks that he has met Jacques before. He is trying to figure out where. Listen to the conversation and fill in the chart with notes about Tony and Jacques.

	Brazil	Venezuela	Argentina	France	Spain
Tony	native country				
Jacques	has never visited				

Pair Practice asking and answering questions about the information in the chart.

Has Jacques ever **visited** Argentina?	Yes, he **has**. / No, he **hasn't**.
Have Tony and Jacques **met** before?	Yes, they **have**. / No, they **haven't**.

Then tell your partner about your own travels.

Have you ever **visited** Taiwan?	Yes, I **have**. I went there two years ago.

2 We've got a lot in common.

Pair Work with your partner to fill in the chart with additional questions about things that you might have in common. Then practice asking and answering the questions.

Have you ever...

Australia

1.	made a snowman?	6.
2.	eaten octopus?	7.
3.	traveled in Australia?	8.
4.	given a speech?	9.
5.	seen a famous person?	10.

Pair Put a check (✔) next to the items that you and your partner have in common. Share your discoveries with the class.

3 Sofia has lived in the United States for about a year.

Pair   Look at the following information about Sofia. Write complete sentences about her. Choose the appropriate verb tense.

Sofia **moved** to Riverside in June.	Sofia **has visited** many places **since** June.
Sofia **bought** a car one month ago.	Sofia **has had** a car **for** one month.
Sofia's English classes **ended** last spring.	Sofia **has not taken** English classes **since** last spring.

1. Sofia/arrive/in Seattle almost one year ago.

   <u>Sofia arrived in Seattle almost a</u>

   <u>year ago.</u>

2. Sofia/not/see/her parents since last year.

   _____

   _____

3. Sofia/move/ to California last Spring.

   _____

   _____

4. Sofia/live/with her aunt and uncle for four months.

   _____

   _____

5. Sofia/met/new friends since she arrived in Riverside.

   _____

   _____

4 I have owned my car for a few years.

Write sentences with *for* and *since* for each picture.

1.

I bought my car in 1998.

I have owned my car for a few years.

I have owned my car since 1998.

2.

It's summer now. Yumiko bought her camera last spring.

_____

_____

3.

It's July. They got married in May.

_____

_____

4.

He found a puppy three days ago.

_____

_____

5 Word Bag: Expressing Understanding

Pair Expressing understanding is an important skill. Look at the following examples and practice them with your partner.

Understand	Don't Understand	Check Understanding
Okay, I get it.	I don't get it.	Am I making any sense?
Yes, I'm with you.	It's not clear to me.	Do you follow me?
I see.	I'm lost.	Are you with me?

Student A: Explain one of the following to your partner. Check to see if your partner understands.

- How to get to your house from here.
- How to make a delicious dish.
- How to operate something such as a computer or a VCR.

Student B: Give your partner feedback on your understanding. Repeat the information to your partner to find out whether you really understood what was being said. Switch roles.

Lesson 2

In this lesson, you will

- introduce yourself and others in a group.
- ask and talk about class rules and regulations.
- describe appropriate classroom behavior.

Nice to meet you, Mr. Robinson.

Listen and read the conversation.

Mr. Robinson: May I help you?

Nelson: Yes, we're looking for our teacher.

Mr. Robinson: Your teacher? What's your teacher's name?

Nelson: Oh, it's on the tip of my tongue. I really should remember it, but I can't right now. Does anybody remember?

Ivan: I don't, but I've heard he's kind of old but a good teacher. Lynn, you should remember his name.

Lynn: Sorry, I can't remember. He taught in Turkey for several years, didn't he?

Nelson: Yes, that's what Mrs. Brennan said.

Mr. Robinson: Is his name Mr. Robinson by any chance?

Lynn: Yes. Mr. Robinson. I remember it now. Can you tell us where we can find him?

Mr. Robinson: Right here. I'm Jerry Robinson, the old but good teacher!

Ivan: Oh, hello Mr. Robinson. How do you do?

Mr. Robinson: I'm fine, thanks. Let me see. You are Ivan, aren't you?

Ivan: Yes, my name is Ivan Gorki. I ought to apologize for my comments.

Mr. Robinson: Don't worry about it.

Ivan: This is Lynn, and this is Nelson.

Nelson: How do you do, sir?

Mr. Robinson: Fine, thank you. Well, nice to meet you all. What can I do for you?

Ivan: We were anxious to meet you, and we wanted to ask you where our classroom is.

Mr. Robinson: Our classroom is Room 245 upstairs. Well, I ought to get going. Have a nice weekend and see you on Monday.

Pair   **Have you ever had an embarrassing moment like Ivan's? What happened? What did you do to get out of the embarrassing situation?**

1 My name's Mr. Robinson.

Pair   It's the first day of class. Mr. Robinson and his students are introducing themselves. Listen to the conversation. Then complete the following chart about the students.

Name	Country	Notes
Yumiko Sato	Japan	likes reading and photography
	Brazil	
		is a new student at the World Language Center; likes writing and sports.
Lynn Wang	China	
	Mali	is interested in cars and loves to play soccer
Jacques Fortier		
Ivan Gorki		likes to go to the gym and loves to eat
	Spain	
		likes scuba diving; has been at the language center for two years

Group   Work in groups of three. Introduce yourself to other group members, and then take turns introducing one of your partners to the other one.

2 You shouldn't eat in class.

Mr. Robinson has made a list of rules for the class. Read the list and put a check (✔) next to the ones you agree or disagree with.

		Agree	Disagree
1.	You should do all your assignments every day.		
2.	You shouldn't copy your classmate's homework.		
3.	You should raise your hand when you have a question.		
4.	You should speak English in class.		
5.	You should respect your classmates.		
6.	You shouldn't ask questions during a test.		
7.	You shouldn't eat in class.		
8.	You should turn off your cellular phone or beeper in class.		
9.	You shouldn't use a dictionary in class.		

Group   Discuss the class rules in your group. Give reasons why you agree or disagree with them.

Example:

I don't agree with number 6. Sometimes a question on a test isn't clear, so I need to ask about it.

3 Can we speak our native language in class?

Ask your teacher questions with *can* or *may* to find out about appropriate classroom behavior. Add two questions of your own.

> **You: Can/May** we **speak** our native language in class?
>
> **Your Teacher:** No, you **can't/may not.** You **can/may** only **speak** English in class.
> OR You **should** only **speak** English in class.

1. call you by your first name
2. speak our native language
3. eat snacks
4. drink water or sodas
5. come to class if we are late

6. use a dictionary in class
7. use a spell-checker in class
8. send you the assignments by e-mail
9. _____
10. _____

Pair   Confirm your teacher's responses by asking your partner questions about the class rules and regulations.

> Can we use a spell-checker in class?
> No, we can't. OR Yes, we can.

4 A good English teacher ought to . . .

Pair   What characteristics do you think a good English teacher *ought to/should* have? Discuss the characteristics below with your partner and number them from 1 (the most important) to 8 (the least important).

A good English teacher ought to/should . . .

_____ know two or more languages.

_____ be able to explain the grammar.

_____ speak slowly and clearly in class.

_____ know students' native language(s).

_____ be patient with students.

_____ teach language and culture together.

_____ return students' homework the next day.

_____ make the class interesting for students.

In your notebook, write a paragraph about two or three characteristics a good English teacher should have. Use *should* or *ought to* in your sentences. Give a reason for each characteristic using *because*.

5 Hear it. Say it.

🔊 Listen to the rhythm and stress in the following questions and answers.

Stress in questions and answers with can/can't

1. Can I have some new checks?   I can only give you three.

2. Can't I have more?   I can't give you more than three.

3. Can you tell us where to find him?   Yes, I can.

4. Can you tell us the new teacher's name?   I can't remember right now.

5. What can I do for you?   You can tell us where our new classroom is.

Pair Practice reading the questions and answers with your partner.

6 May I help you?

🔊 Sofia, a new student at the World Language Center, is in the library speaking with the clerk at the Circulation Desk. Listen to the conversation. Then, check (✔) the items that Sofia has with her.

1. ___ driver's license
2. ___ change
3. ___ credit card
4. ___ dollar bill
5. ___ library card
6. ___ student ID
7. ___ cellular phone

Pair What is Sofia's problem? Have you ever been in a situation like Sofia's? Tell your partner what happened and how you resolved your problem.

7 Role-play

Pair Work with a partner. Write a dialog for one of the following situations. Use *may* or *can* to ask for permission or to request something.

Example: (*at the bank*)

A: May I help you?

B: Yes, please. Can I have some new checks?

A: I can only give you three.

B: But I have to pay all my bills.

A: You have to request new checks by mail. I can't give you more than three.

1. at a bookstore

2. at the post office

3. at the school registration office

4. at the supermarket

Lesson 3

In this lesson, you will
- discuss cultural adaptation.
- express conclusions.

When Home Is a World Away

🔊 **Listen and read the following conversation.**

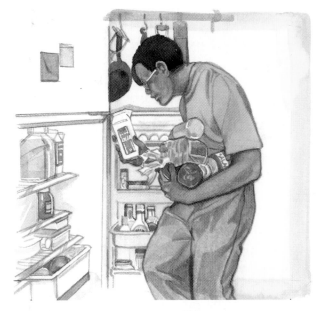

Nelson: You know when you invited us to your house the other night, Mr. Robinson?

Mr. Robinson: Yes.

Nelson: Something happened that I don't really understand. Can I ask you about it?

Mr. Robinson: Of course, Nelson. What is it?

Nelson: You asked me if I wanted more meat, and I said no.

Mr. Robinson: So?

Nelson: But you didn't ask me again.

Mr. Robinson: Well, I thought you must be full or you mustn't like meat.

Nelson: No, I was still very hungry and meat is one of my favorite foods.

Mr. Robinson: So why didn't you accept another helping?

Nelson: But that would be very rude. In my country, I would refuse the offer.

Mr. Robinson: Well, in the United States when you refuse, we assume you must not want any more.

Nelson: In my culture, you wouldn't just offer it to me once or twice. You might insist many times, but I would still refuse.

Mr. Robinson: Really? For me, it wouldn't be polite to insist many times.

Nelson: I didn't know that. Now I understand what happened.

Mr. Robinson: I'm glad you asked about it. You must be relieved to know that I wasn't being rude.

Nelson: Oh, yes I am. But I still raided the refrigerator when I got home.

Pair Have you ever lived in another town, city, or country? What cultural differences did you experience? Was it difficult for you to adapt? Easy? Tell your partner about it.

1 The Whole Picture

Pair Here's part of a picture. Guess what it is and what the person might be doing. Then turn to page 25 to see the whole picture.

2 He must not be very happy.

Pair Look at the following pictures. Write conclusions using *must* or *must not* and the words in brackets.

1. [very happy]

Nelson got a 55 on his English test. <u>He must not be very</u> <u>happy.</u>

2. [tired]

Gina studied all night. _____ _____

3. [interested]

The students are falling asleep. _____ _____

4. [homesick]

Yumiko hasn't heard from her family. _____ _____

5. [well]

Tony hasn't eaten anything all day. _____ _____

6. [lost]

Mr. Robinson hasn't arrived at school. _____ _____

3 They must like jazz.

Group Look at the picture. What logical conclusions can you make about the people who live in the apartment? Discuss with your group, and then write three to five sentences about them. Share your conclusions with the class.

> There are two empty pizza boxes on the table.
>
> They **must like** pizza.

The Whole Picture

The person is a construction worker on a high-rise building in New York City. Today, women are doing jobs that used to be seen as "men's jobs." Can you name some other occupations that are traditionally thought of as being "for men only"? What do you think about women and men doing the same jobs?

4 Online

Log onto **http://www.prenhall.com/brown_activities**
The Web: Comparative Education
Grammar: What's your grammar IQ?
E-mail: Time for a Change

5 Wrap Up

Group Look at the following picture. What does the caption mean? Does the man on the left look like he's having a good time? Why not? Discuss what he could do to feel more comfortable. What would you do?

When in Rome, do as the Romans do.

Strategies for Success

➤ Practicing communication strategies
➤ Identifying behaviors for successful language learning
➤ Understanding cultural stereotypes

1. With a Learning Partner, look at Lesson 1, Exercise 5 and add some more phrases for understanding someone in a conversation. You may think of expressions like: "uh-huh," "Sorry, what did you say?" or "You know what I mean?" Then, do some more practice using those phrases in the conversation below (#2).

2. With a partner, brainstorm some "classroom behaviors" that are especially helpful in learning English, specifically. You may want to list things like: listening to the teacher's directions carefully, raising your hand to volunteer answers or to ask questions, making sure you know the purpose of a task, etc. Write your list in your journal. Copy the list onto a bright-colored card or paper and put it on your bulletin board or some place where you will see it every day.

3. With your partner, brainstorm some stereotypes of several cultures or countries you are both familiar with (for example, "Americans are rich and friendly." "Japanese are smart and polite.") Decide whether the stereotypes are really true or not. Remember to practice the conversation strategies you discussed above.

CHECKPOINT

How much have you learned in this unit? Review the goals for each lesson. What skills can you confidently use now? What skills do you need to practice? List these below.

Skills I've Learned Well

_____

_____

_____

_____

Skills I Need to Practice

_____

_____

_____

_____

Learning Preferences

In this unit, which type of activity did you like the best and the least? Write the number in the box: 1 = best; 2 = next best; 3 = next; 4 = least.

❑ Working by myself   ❑ Working with a group

❑ Working with a partner   ❑ Working as a whole class

In this unit, which exercises helped you to learn to:

listen more effectively?   Exercise ____   read more easily?   Exercise ____

speak more fluently?   Exercise ____   write more clearly?   Exercise ____

Which exercise did you like the most? ____   Why? _____

Which exercise did you like the least? ____   Why? _____

VOCABULARY

Nouns
cellular phone
construction worker
high-rise building
lifestyle

Regular Verbs
apologize
exchange
improve
raid

Irregular Verbs
buy-bought-bought
eat-ate-eaten
find-found-found
give-gave-given
meet-met-met
see-saw-seen
speak-spoke-spoken
take-took-taken

Clarifying information
I get it.
I'm with you.
I see.
I don't get it.
It's not clear to me.
I'm lost.
Am I making any sense?
Do you follow me?
Are you with me?

GRAMMAR SUMMARY

MODALS

Asking for permission

May I **use** a dictionary during the test?
Can she **send** assignments by e-mail?

Giving permission

No, you **may not use** it during the test.
Sure, she **can send** assignments by e-mail.

Asking for advice

Should I **speak** only English in class?
What **should** he **do** to improve his teaching?

Giving advice

Yes, you **should** only **speak** English in class.
He **ought to speak** slowly and clearly.

Expressing conclusions

He **must not be** very happy.
She **must** like pizza.

SIMPLE PAST *VS.* PRESENT PERFECT

Finished time

I **studied** English in elementary school.
Tony **took** classes here last year.
They **did not place** me **yesterday**.
Did you **visit** Argentina?

Unfinished time

I **have studied** English **since** I was a child.
He **has taken** classes here **for** a year.
They **have not placed** me **yet**.
Have you **ever visited** Argentina?

COMMUNICATION SUMMARY

Exchanging information about personal history
I've studied English since I was a child.
She hasn't seen her family for many months.
Talking about yourself and your experiences
I have never eaten octopus.
Expressing understanding or lack of understanding
I get it.
I don't get it.
Clarifying information
Am I making sense?

Introducing yourself and others
How do you do?
Fine, thank you.
This is Lynn, and this is Nelson.
It's nice to meet you.
Asking and talking about appropriate classroom behavior
Can I eat snacks in class?
No, you can't. You should eat before you come to class.
Expressing conclusions
They must be hungry.
He must not be very happy.

UNIT 3

Lesson 1

In this lesson, you will
- confirm information.
- talk about the past.

Across Generations

🎧 **Listen and read.**

Gina: Sometimes I think my parents and I speak a different language.

Tony: Of course you do. You're speaking English now, and they speak Italian.

Gina: Seriously. We used to have a wonderful relationship. Now it seems that everything I do bothers them.

Tony: In what way?

Gina: Well, they say I spend too much time talking on the telephone. And definitely too much money on clothes.

Tony: Oh, Gina. You haven't been shopping again, have you?

Mr. Robinson: This is definitely a case of the Generation Gap.

Gina: Generation Gap?

Mr. Robinson: Yes, younger and older generations live in distinct worlds. When young people try to become independent, they feel almost obliged to disagree with their elders. And the adults don't understand this behavior.

Tony: We've all experienced this, haven't we? My 15-year-old brother contradicts everything my father says. Then my father gets mad and they argue.

Mr. Robinson: Well, when I was 15, I used to think my father was the least intelligent man in the world. By the time I reached 20, however, I was amazed how much the old man had learned!

Gina: You've also learned a lot since then, haven't you, Mr. Robinson?

<u>Pair</u>   **What causes some of the problems between the older and younger generations? Do you think Mr. Robinson bridged the Generation Gap? Explain.**

1 Senior citizens value hard work.

Read the following information about four different generations in the United States.

Senior Citizens
People born before 1942 experienced the Great Depression, World War II, and the Cold War. They value hard work, duty, and sacrifice.

Baby Boomers
People born between 1943 and 1963 experienced a strong economy, color television, and rock 'n' roll. They are concerned about social causes and the environment. They value self-improvement through education, diet, and exercise.

Generation Xers
People born between 1964 and 1984 grew up with video games and personal computers. They value independence, and they're not afraid to take risks.

Millennials
People born after 1984 grew up with CDs, cellular phones, and the Internet. They value technology and are optimistic about the future.

Pair   Do different generations in your country have distinct characteristics? Explain. Are there names for the different generations? Which generation do you belong to?

2 Gina, you haven't been shopping again, have you?

We**'ve** all experienced this before, **haven't we?**	She**'s used** a computer before, **hasn't she?**
You **haven't been** shopping again, **have you?**	He **hasn't used** one, **has he?**

Group   Ask other students some tag questions about themselves.

Example:

A: You've used a computer before, haven't you?

B: No, I haven't.

A: You aren't afraid to use one, are you?

B: No, I'm not.

3 Hear it. Say it.

Listen to the following questions. Is the speaker fairly sure of the answer or is he or she unsure? Check *sure* or *unsure*.

Tag Questions

1. Many teenagers argue with their parents, don't they?   ( ) sure   ( ) unsure

2. It's your first day in this school, isn't it?   ( ) sure   ( ) unsure

3. They've done it before, haven't they?   ( ) sure   ( ) unsure

4. You haven't paid cash, have you?   ( ) sure   ( ) unsure

Pair   Take turns asking the questions. Your partner will tell you whether you sound sure or unsure about the answer.

4 The Good Old Days

Look at the photograph and guess when it was taken. Then listen as Mr. Robinson continues his conversation with Tony and Gina.

Mr. Robinson: I grew up in the 1950s in a small town in the Midwest.

Tony: Where is the Midwest, Mr. Robinson? Around Chicago?

Mr. Robinson: Yes. Chicago is the big city of the Midwest, just like New York is the big city of the East.

Tony: But you didn't live in the big city, did you?

Mr. Robinson: No, I lived in a small, quiet town north of Chicago. I always think of my childhood as "the good old days."

Gina: But it wasn't that long ago, Mr. Robinson. I always think "the good old days" were about a hundred years ago.

Mr. Robinson: I understand what you mean, Gina, but to me, the 1950s in this country seem like a hundred years ago. Times have changed so fast!

Gina: Oh, I see what you mean–home computers, cellular phones, even color television didn't exist yet, did they?

Mr. Robinson: No, not yet. We had a simple life, and it seems like a long time ago.

Pair   Discuss with your partner why Mr. Robinson thinks of the days of his childhood as "the good old days." Then report your opinions to the class.

5 Families used to live in one place for a long time.

People **used to** get married young.	**Did** teen boys **use to** wear their hair long?
Most women **didn't use to** work.	Girls **used to** wear short skirts, **didn't** they?

<u>Pair</u>   **Complete the sentences with *used to*, *didn't use to*, or the simple past tense.**

The early 1950s in the United States was a time of traditional values, such as commitment and family identity. People _____used to get_____ married young and most women
(1. get)
_____ home and _____ care
(2. stay)   (3. take)
of their children. Families _____ from one place
(4. not/move)
to another very often.

In contrast, the late fifties and sixties were a time of changing fashions as well as social and political change. Young people _____the twist,
(5. do)
and children _____ with Barbie® dolls,
(6. play)
skateboards, and hula hoops. Teen boys _____
(7. have)
long hair, and teen girls _____ their skirts either
(8. wear)
very short or very long.

Many adults _____ the clothes, lifestyle, and
(9. criticize)
music of the younger generation. A new term, "the generation gap," was used to explain the difference between adults and young people.

<u>Group</u>   **Discuss how life used to be in your country in the 1950s. Then compare it with how it is now. Finally, predict what life will be like in twenty years.**

Lesson 2

In this lesson, you will

- express your opinions.
- express goals.
- write a letter defending your opinion.
- identify the main idea.

A Woman of Science

🎧 **Listen and read the article.**

Mina Goldman has just come back from an early morning walk on the beach. At 82, she moves as briskly as a woman of 20. Dr. Goldman has just completed her tenth book, *Morning Shadows*, in which she describes her life as one of the first women to enter the field of genetic engineering. On this busy morning, she has only a short time to talk with Heidi Wright, our science correspondent, before she makes an appearance at a local high school.

HW: Dr. Goldman, why haven't more women chosen careers in science?

MG: Well, first of all, most children grow up with the idea that boys understand science more easily than girls do. This continues in the high school and college years. Later, it's hard for a woman to get a job in science.

HW: I see. The culture doesn't encourage women to become scientists.

MG: Exactly. Young women give up on science more quickly than boys do because they feel embarrassed. They think science belongs to boys.

HW: How have you managed to escape this way of thinking?

MG: I think it began with my mother. She always believed in my ability, and I've tried to make her proud. Now I get paid to do science, so I guess it worked.

HW: You've never married. Did you sacrifice a family for your work?

MG: (*laughs*) Well, no, I didn't. I'm single by choice. A career doesn't get in the way. I know many women scientists who are happily married and have families.

HW: That's good to know. And are you happy with your life?

MG: I am. I've enjoyed myself, and I hope that I've set an example for other women. Science is for everyone.

Pair **What fields are traditionally male and what fields are traditionally female in your culture? Explain to your partner why you think this is the case.**

1 Senior citizens participate more actively.

Dr. Goldman is making a great contribution in the field of science at an age when most Americans are retired. What is the lifestyle of older people in your country? Compare your country to the United States. Check where you think each statement is true.

	Your Country	The United States
1. Seniors participate more actively in family life.		
2. Seniors live more independently.		
3. Seniors are treated more respectfully.		
4. Seniors exercise less often.		
5. Seniors watch their diet less carefully.		
6. Seniors see their children less frequently.		

2 Are boys less cautious than girls?

There are many generalizations about the talents and skills of boys and girls. Fill in the correct form of the adverb, and then circle *more* or *less* according to what you think.

1. Boys are more/less *decisive* than girls are. They make decisions more/less _____decisively_____ than girls do.

2. Girls are more/less *cooperative* than boys are. They work together more/less _____ than boys do.

3. Boys are more/less *patient* than girls are. They deal with problems more/less _____ than girls do.

4. Girls are more/less *logical* than boys are. They think more/less _____ than boys do.

5. Girls are more/less *creative* than boys are. They find solutions more/less _____ than boys do.

6. Boys are more/less *cautious* than girls are. They behave more/less _____ than girls do.

7. (Write one of your own.) _____

Class Discuss your choices with the other students.

3 Word Bag: Expressing Opinions.

Pair   Share your opinions about the following topics. Use the model below.

What do you think about women in science?	Personally, I think that they can/can't be good scientists.
In your opinion, can men and women do all of the same things?	Actually, I believe women can/can't do heavy construction work as well as men can.
What's your opinion of separate schools for girls and boys?	I am in favor of/against separate schools for girls and boys.

- Mothers who work

- Women soldiers

- People in their 80s who work full time

- Other _____

4 I would like to be more patient than I am now.

Pair   These people are setting goals for themselves. Look at the pictures below and on page 36. Write a sentence with the adverb. Then check your answers with a partner.

She wants to be **more patient than** she is.	She should speak **more patiently than** she does now.
I want to have a **less expensive** lifestyle.	I want to live **less expensively**.

carefully

1. Jacques needs to be more careful.

clearly

2. Dr. Goldman wants to be clearer when she speaks.

honestly

seriously

3. Pablo wants to be more honest.

4. Ivan would like to be a more serious student.

1. <u>Jacques should ride his bike more carefully than he does now.</u>

2. _____

3. _____

4. _____

5 Is Mina Goldman inspiring or irresponsible?

Read the following opinion letters about Mina Goldman's interview.

Dear Editor,

I loved your interview with Mina Goldman in last week's issue. <u>I think it's important for girls to learn about successful women.</u> I gave the article to my daughters to read, and they have not stopped talking about it.

Dorothy Carson,
Riverside, CA

Dear Editor,

Your interview with Mina Goldman gives girls the wrong impression. It's wrong to let young women think that they can be good mothers and successful scientists at the same time. They can't. I know, because when I got married and had children, I did not have time for my career. I think Dr. Goldman knows it's impossible, but she doesn't want to admit it.

Terry Hanson,
Pasadena, CA

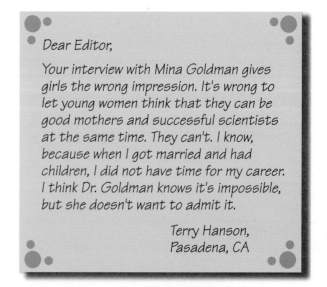

Pair Discuss the two letters. What is each writer's opinion? Look at the underlined sentence in Dorothy Carson's letter. That is her main idea. Underline the sentence that expresses the main idea in Terry Hanson's letter, and compare your answer with your partner's.

Lesson 3

In this lesson, you will
- read for specific information.
- arrange events in chronological order.
- write a definition of a hero.

Nelson Mandela

Listen and read.

NEWSLETTER

Nelson Rolihlahla Mandela was born on July 18, 1918 in a village in South Africa. After his father argued with an important white official, Nelson's mother took him to another village. When he was 7, his parents sent him to a missionary school. There he was given his English name, Nelson. Two years later, his father died, and Nelson went to live with his uncle. This man strongly influenced the future president's leadership style.

When Mandela entered college in 1939, he participated in activities against the South African government. He also managed to do well academically, earned a law degree, and was on the road to a comfortable life. However, his experience and education had taught him about injustice in his country. In 1943, he joined the African National Congress (ANC).

In 1948, the government passed the apartheid laws. These laws generally treated non-whites as inferior citizens. As an active member of the ANC, Mandela played a major role in protesting against these laws. He was arrested in 1956, and then again eight years later. The second time, the apartheid police found arms in the headquarters of Mandela's organization and he was sentenced to life in prison.

For twenty-eight years, Mandela remained in prison. Finally, in 1990 President F. W. de Klerk released him from prison, and allowed

him to return to his work with the ANC. Three years later, both Mandela and de Klerk were awarded the Nobel Peace Prize for their efforts to end apartheid and bring about a peaceful transition to nonracial democracy in South Africa. In 1994, Mandela was elected president of South Africa.

Mandela fought all his life to bring freedom to black people and democracy to his country. He's known as a national hero in his country and abroad. He served as president of South Africa until 1999, when he stepped down after serving for five years.

Source: Based on information in *Nelson Mandela: The Man and the Movement* by Mary Benson, W.W. Norton & Company, Inc., 1986 and *Nelson Mandela: The Fight Against Apartheid* by Steven Otfinoski, The Millbrook Press, 1992.

Pair **Do you think Nelson Mandela is a hero? Why? Is there a national hero in your country? Why is he or she considered a hero?**

1 What did Nelson Mandela fight against?

Information	Question
His birthdate	When was Mandela born?

Write questions with *Who? What? Where? When? Why?* or *How long?*

Information	Question
1. The place where he was born	
2. The person he lived with after his father died	
3. The year he joined the African National Congress	
4. The reason he was sentenced to life in prison	
5. The number of years he was in prison	
6. The reason he won the Nobel Peace Prize	
7. The year he was elected president of South Africa	

Class Read your questions aloud for other students to answer.

2 Nelson Mandela was a hero.

Pair Read the following statements from Nelson Mandela's biography again. Then circle the letter of the sentence that has the same meaning.

1. There he was given his English name, Nelson.
   a. When Nelson's mother took him to another village, he was given the name Nelson.
   b. Nelson's name was Rolihlahla before he went to missionary school.

2. Two years later, his father died, and Nelson went to live with his uncle.
   a. Nelson never lived with his mother after his father died.
   b. Right after his father died, Nelson went to live with his uncle.

3. The second time, the apartheid police found arms in the headquarters of Mandela's organization, and he was sentenced to life in prison.
   a. When Mandela was arrested in 1964, he was given a life sentence.
   b. Mandela was sent to prison twice for protesting against the apartheid laws.

4. Finally, in 1990, President F. W. de Klerk released him from prison, and allowed him to return to his work with the ANC.
   a. Before Mandela went to prison, he was working with the ANC.
   b. Mandela started to work for the ANC after he was released from prison in 1990.

3 Ordinary heroes live among us.

Pair Listen to the story from a radio show called *We live among heroes*. Then number the events in chronological order from 1 to 7.

On a September day in 1951, a ten-year-old boy and a nine-year-old girl rode their bikes to the bank of a river.

Parker braced his knee against a tree and caught Jerry by her injured right arm. _____

Parker gave Jerry a ride on his bike.

An alligator came out of the water and grasped Jerry by the arm.

The alligator came out of the water, and for a few seconds, lost its grip on the girl's arm.

Jerry and Parker rode their bikes to the bank of a river.

Jerry was taken to the hospital in a truck.

Parker was proclaimed a hero.

Class Discuss what you think you might do in a similar situation.

4 Online

Log onto **http://www.prenhall.com/brown_activities**
The Web: The Contributions of Senior Citizens
Grammar: What's your grammar IQ?
E-mail: So much has changed!

5 Wrap Up

Group **Look at the following dictionary definition of a hero.**

Source: *Longman Dictionary of English Language and Culture*

hero/herr 632

hero (hir´ō; *also* hē´rō)
Someone who is admired for his or her bravery, goodness, or great ability, especially someone who has performed an act of great courage under very dangerous conditions.

Discuss the definition with your group and answer the following questions.

1. Do you agree with the dictionary definition of a hero?

2. Do you think a hero has to be famous?

3. Do you have a personal hero in your life? Why do you think of that person as a hero? What has that person done or achieved in her or his life?

4. Write your definition of a hero.

Strategies for Success

➤ **Expressing opinions**
➤ **Interviewing, taking notes, and writing based on notes**
➤ **Complimenting and encouraging yourself**

1. With a Learning Partner, discuss your opinions on how we should solve the following problems: (1) conserving the earth's natural resources; (2) employers preferring to hire younger workers; and (3) violence in movies and on TV. In your discussion, use the expressions you learned in this chapter for expressing opinions.

2. Interview your partner in order to find out many things about your partner's life. Take notes. Then, using your notes, write a biographical paragraph about your partner. Try to use the vocabulary you learned in this unit (see the list at the end of the unit).

3. In your journal, write about the things that you do well in English. Be as specific and detailed as possible ("I am good at taking multiple-choice tests."). Share these thoughts with a partner and ask if the partner agrees with you.

CHECKPOINT

How much have you learned in this unit? Review the goals for each lesson. What skills can you confidently use now? What skills do you need to practice? List these below.

Skills I've Learned Well

_____

_____

_____

_____

Skills I Need to Practice

_____

_____

_____

_____

Learning Preferences

In this unit, which type of activity did you like the best and the least? Write the number in the box: 1 = best; 2 = next best; 3 = next; 4 = least.

❑ Working by myself   ❑ Working with a group

❑ Working with a partner   ❑ Working as a whole class

In this unit, which exercises helped you to learn to:

listen more effectively?   Exercise _____   read more easily?   Exercise _____

speak more fluently?   Exercise _____   write more clearly?   Exercise _____

Which exercise did you like the most? _____   Why? _____

Which exercise did you like the least? _____   Why? _____

VOCABULARY

Nouns	Adjectives	Adverbs	To Share Opinions
behavior	cautious	definitely	What do you think about . . .
childhood	cooperative	frequently	I think/believe that . . .
generation	confident	honestly	In your opinion . . .
relationship	creative	independently	I have mixed feelings about . . .
	decisive	intelligently	I am against/in favor of . . .
Verbs	distinct	respectfully	What's your opinion of . . .
argue	logical	scientifically	
bother	obliged	seriously	
contradict	optimistic		
disagree	patient		
experience	responsible		

▶ GRAMMAR SUMMARY

Present Perfect Tag Questions

She's **used** a computer before, **hasn't she?**	We've all **experienced** this before, **haven't** we?
He **hasn't used** one, **has he?**	You **haven't been** shopping again, **have** you?

Used to

People **used to** get married young.	**Did** teen boys **use to** wear their hair long?
Most women **didn't use** to work.	Girls **used to** wear short skirts, **didn't** they?

Comparison of adjectives and adverbs

I want to be **more patient** than I am.	I should speak **more patiently** than I do.
Dr. Goldman wants to be **clearer** when she speaks.	She wants to speak **more clearly**.

Wh-questions

When was Mandela born?	**Why** did he go to live with his uncle?
Where did he go to school?	**How long** was he in jail?
Who did he live with?	**What** did he fight against?

▶ COMMUNICATION SUMMARY

Confirming information
She's used a computer before, hasn't she?

Talking about the past
We used to have a wonderful relationship.

Expressing opinions
I think women can be good scientists.
I am against separate schools for girls.

Expressing goals
I want to be more patient than I am now.
She would like to speak more clearly.

Identifying main ideas
It's wrong to let young women think that they can be good mothers and successful scientists.

Writing a definition
A hero is a person who is famous for something brave or good.

Reading for specific information
Mandela was born on July 18, 1918.
He was born in a village in South Africa.

Lesson 1

In this lesson, you will:
- describe a sequence of events in the past.
- write a journal entry.
- ask for and give reasons.

Anatomy of an Illness

🔊 **Listen and read Oscar's journal.**

Monday, March 24 —I've been sneezing and coughing for about a week now. At first it wasn't so bad, and I thought maybe it was just a cold. But I had to take some aspirin before I went to bed because I had a fever and chills, a sore throat, and an earache, too.

Tuesday, March 25 —Today I got up feeling worse, because the cough was constant and I had a terrible headache. But after I took some cough syrup, I went to school. After I was there for an hour or so, I was too sick to do anything, and I had to go home. When I got home, I fell into bed and slept most of the day. Tomorrow, I'm going to see Dr. Lei.

Wednesday, March 26—Well, Dr. Lei said it wasn't just a cold because I had a sore throat and a fever, too. He took a blood test and when the lab results came back, they showed I had a really bad bacterial infection. The doctor prescribed an antibiotic and told me to stay in bed for a couple of days and drink a lot of fluids, especially hot beverages.

Saturday, March 29—Today was a wonderful day because my fever was gone and I wasn't coughing anymore. The hot drinks really helped my sore throat. When Lynn called to ask how I was feeling, I was finally able to say, "A lot better!"

Pair   Do you seek treatment only when you become ill or do you try to prevent illness and maintain your health? Discuss with your partner the ways you take care of your health.

1 When I got home, I fell into bed.

I **had** to take some aspirin **before** I **went** to bed. I **was** too sick to do anything **after** I **was** there for an hour. I **fell** into bed when I **got** home.	**Before** I **went** to bed, I **had** to take some aspirin. **After** I **was** there for an hour, I **was** too sick to do anything. **When** I **got** home, I **fell** into bed.

Pair   Read each pair of sentences below. Combine them into one sentence using *before*, *after*, or *when*. More than one answer is possible for each pair of sentences.

Example:

They took a blood test. They found he had an infection.
When they took a blood test, **they found** he had an infection.

1. He had the cough for a week.
    He went to the doctor.

2. He took an antibiotic. He felt better.

3. He got very sick.
    He had to go home.

4. He went home. He stopped at the drugstore.

2 Dr. Lei had a busy day yesterday.

Pair   Dr. Lei had a busy day yesterday. Look at his schedule and talk about it, using *before*, *after*, or *when*.

After he **finished** the surgery, he **made** his morning rounds.

DAILY PLANNER

			Wednesday, March 26
7:00	perform surgery	3:00	see patients at clinic
10:00	make morning rounds, update patients' charts	5:30	interview new medical assistant
12:00	have lunch	7:00	make evening rounds
1:00	lecture at Medical School	8:00	attend meeting of Medical Association, vote on new members
2:00	correct student papers		

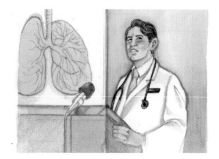

3 Because he got sick, he missed his classes.

Effect	Cause
He **missed** his classes	**because** he **got** sick.

Cause	Effect
Because he **got** sick,	he **missed** his classes.

Pair Read Anatomy of an Illness again. Find four sentences showing cause and effect. Write the sentences in your notebook. Circle the cause in each sentence.

4 Step on the scales, please.

Pair Match the command with what the doctor wants to do. Then ask and answer questions.

Example:

    A: **Why** did you open your mouth?   B: **Because** the doctor wanted to look at my throat.

1. Open your mouth.
2. Step on the scales.
3. Take a deep breath.
4. Read the last line of the eye chart.
5. Put the thermometer in your mouth.

_____ Listen to my heart and lungs.
_____ Measure my weight and height.
_____ Take my temperature.
__1_ Look at my throat.
_____ Check my eyes.

5 Yesterday I wasn't feeling very well.

Pair Listen and complete Oscar's journal entry.

> Dear Diary,
>
>   Yesterday I wasn't feeling very well. I had a _____ and _____, and my _____ was aching, too. After I had breakfast, I decided to go to _____. When I got there, I had to wait a long time because _____. Before I saw Doctor Lei, I had to _____.
>
>   *(continued)*

After he _____ my temperature, Doctor Lei told me to roll up my sleeve because he wanted to _____. He said I had _____. He told me to stay in bed and _____. Before I went home, I stopped by the pharmacy because _____. After I got home, I _____. I'm really glad I went to see the doctor, because I am feeling _____ now.

6 Word Bag: Talking about Health

Pair Read and discuss the expressions below. Practice saying them out loud.

A: You look a little **run down**.
B: I'm just feeling a bit **under the weather**.

A: You're sweating. Are you **running a fever?**
B: Yes, but I'm sure that it will **go away** soon.

A: I guess your cold **took a turn for the worse**.
B: Yes, the symptoms **came back**.

A: **Take care of yourself. Get plenty of rest.**
B: You'll **get better** soon.
A: Good. So you think I'll **pull through**?

Pair Rewrite the following conversation replacing the *italicized* words or phrases with some of the expressions above.

Oscar: When is this cold going to stop? I hate being sick.

Lynn: You look *very tired. Do you have a high temperature?*

Oscar: Well, I did, but it's close to normal now. I *stayed in bed and rested* for a couple of days. I thought I was better, but then yesterday, my cold symptoms *got worse*. The fever stayed down though.

Lynn: I guess these things take a while.

Oscar: Yes, don't worry though. I'll *be healthy* soon.

Lynn: I know. You'll *recover*. Get some rest. You don't want the infection to *return* for the weekend!

Interview your partner about the last time he or she got sick. Then use some of the expressions above to tell the class about his or her illness.

Lesson 2

In this lesson, you will:
- discuss a visit to an emergency room.
- report direct speech.
- understand a hospital bill.

He said, "It's just indigestion."

Nelson and Sofia are visiting Gina. She was sick and didn't go to school yesterday. Listen and read their conversation.

Nelson: How are you feeling, Gina? I heard you had a bad stomachache yesterday.

Gina: Yes, but I feel better today, thanks.

Sofia: Did you see a doctor?

Gina: Yes, I went to the emergency room. After he examined me, the doctor said, "It's just indigestion. Here's a prescription for some pills. You'll be fine by tomorrow."

Nelson: And you are better today.

Gina: Yes, I'm fine.

Sofia: Did you see your regular doctor at the emergency room?

Gina: No, I saw the doctor who was on duty.

Nelson: You do have a regular doctor though, don't you?

Gina: Yes, I have a primary-care physician.

Sofia: Is that like a family doctor?

Gina: Yes, it is. But I was in so much pain the other day, I just went right to the emergency room. It was a real emergency!

Nelson: I guess it was!

Pair **What kind of medical care do you have? Tell your partner about it.**

1 The receptionist asked, "How can I help you?"

Pair Look at each picture and tell your partner what each person said.

Example:

The receptionist **asked, "How can I help you**?"
Lynn **said, "My friend needs to see a doctor right away."**

Lynn: My friend has to see the doctor immediately.
Receptionist: Has she filled out the form?

Doctor: When did your stomachache start?
Gina: Last night.

Doctor: What did you eat, Gina?
Gina: I ate a steak and some french fries.

Gina: When should I take these pills?
Pharmacist: Take them just before your meals.

2 The doctor said, "You'll be fine. Don't worry."

Pair When Gina's stomachache got worse, Lynn took her to the emergency room at the hospital. Look at the following statements and guess who said each one. Choose from the box.

| Lynn   doctor   pharmacist   receptionist |

1. **The doctor** said, "You'll be fine. Don't worry!"

2. _____ said, "I can pick up your medicine."

3. _____ asked, "Are you on any medication right now?"

4. _____ said, "I need to copy your insurance card."

5. _____ said, "Roll up your sleeve. I need to take your blood pressure."

6. _____ said, "Take one pill before each meal."

7. _____ asked, "What did the doctor tell you?"

8. _____ said, "The doctor will be with you shortly."

9. _____ asked, "Does it hurt when I press here?"

3 Hear it. Say it.

Listen to the sentences. Draw a slash (/) between the two thought groups in each sentence. Practice saying the sentences with a partner.

1. Before I went home, I got sick.

2. When he took an antibiotic, he felt better.

3. After he operated, he saw patients.

4. Because he got sick, he missed his classes.

5. Because I had a fever, I took some aspirin.

6. Because the fever was gone, I had a wonderful day.

4 My Visit to the Doctor

Gina is writing in her journal about her visit to the emergency room. Listen and complete her journal entry.

Last week I had a horrible stomachache. The pain woke me up in the middle of the night and I couldn't go back to sleep. Early in the morning, I went to the emergency room at the hospital. I had to wait for an hour before it was my turn. While I was waiting, the receptionist gave me several forms to fill out. When it was finally my turn, a nurse came and said, "_____1_____!" As I followed the nurse to the examining room, she asked, "_____2_____?" "I need to _____3_____ immediately," I said. "The doctor will _____4_____," the nurse responded with a smile.

As soon as the doctor came into the examination room, he asked, "_____5_____?" I answered, "I have a _____6_____." "A stomachache," he repeated what I'd said, and then asked, "_____7_____?" "_____8_____," I responded. "What did you eat last night?" "_____9_____" I said, "oh and a few french fries." Then, he said, "_____10_____." I untucked my shirt. He felt my stomach and asked where it hurt. Finally, he wrote a prescription. He handed it to me, and said, "_____11_____. Get this prescription filled. The pills will help right away." "_____12_____?" I said, "That's good! I thought it was something serious."

5 I have some questions about the bill.

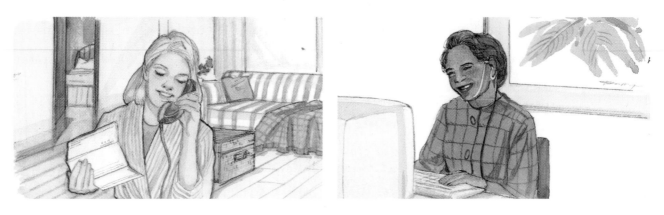 Gina has some questions about the bill she received from the hospital. Listen to the telephone conversation and fill in the missing information.

MERCY HOSPITAL EMERGENCY SERVICES

Patient Number			DATE	
Patient Name GINA POGGI				

Medical Coverage: **Multi-Health-Care Providers**   Group Number: **943-2076**

Type of Service Provided	Service Dates	Amt Charged	Insurance Cover	Deductible	TOTAL PAID	BALANCE DUE
Doctor Visit		55.00	40.00		40.00	$15.00
GASTRIL 500	10-24-01	15.00		00.00	00.00	15.00*
					TOTAL DUE:	**$30.00** *not covered by insurance

Lesson 3

In this lesson, you will

- demonstrate understanding of medicine labels.
- discuss health insurance and how it works.
- scan for specific information.
- discuss the relationship between lifestyle and health.

Guaranteed: Instant Relief

Group Review the medicine labels and discuss which remedies you would recommend for the situations illustrated on page 52. Would you recommend one of the medicines described here or some other remedy you know about?

Ezsleep **Warning:** Ask your doctor about Ezsleep if you have a breathing problem such as emphysema or chronic bronchitis. In case of accidental overdose, contact a poison control center immediately. Possible side effects include drowsiness and headache.

Awake **Warning:** If tiredness persists, consult your doctor. The caffeine in Awake may cause nervousness, irritability and rapid heartbeat. If you are pregnant, consult your doctor before using this product.

Tension Tabs **Warning:** Do not take more than recommended dosage. Avoid alcohol while taking this product. If dizziness or upset stomach occurs, stop use and call your doctor. Keep out of reach of children.

A long-time smoker has emphysema. He has difficulty sleeping, but he also has trouble breathing. What is your recommendation?

A young man is falling asleep in the back of the class. He's slightly unkempt and it's obvious he hasn't slept all night. What is your recommendation?

An employee has been working long hours at the company. The manager is happy, but he has recently noticed that the employee has been arguing with coworkers and seems to get angry more easily than usual. What do you think he should do?

A student has become so nervous about a test that now he can't even sit down and study. What should he do to relax?

1 Exercise is as stimulating as a cup of coffee.

Read the following statements and write _yes_ next to the statements that you agree with and _no_ next to statements you disagree with.

_____ 1. Sitting at home is not as helpful as going for a walk when you feel stress.

_____ 2. Watching an exciting movie is as soothing as a hot bath when you need to get some sleep.

_____ 3. Exercise is just as important as a healthy diet when you need energy.

_____ 4. Watching a comedy show on TV is not as effective as listening to quiet music when you are feeling anxious.

_____ 5. Getting a good night's sleep is not as important as studying before a test.

_____ 6. When you are tired, a brisk walk is more stimulating than a cup of coffee.

Class   **On the board, make a chart of the number of students who answered _yes_ to each statement. When you finish, look at the numbers and see if there is class agreement.**

2 Health Insurance in the United States

<u>Group</u> In the United States, managed health care was developed to prevent medical treatment from becoming too expensive. Look at the following descriptions of three kinds of health insurance offered in the United States. Then share your opinions about the questions that follow.

Lynn's cousin Betty belongs to a Health Management Organization called an HMO. When Betty gets sick, she goes to the clinic and sees one of the doctors who works there. She doesn't have a personal doctor, but one of a group of doctors that includes many specialists. The HMO chooses her physician for her. She pays a small fee (usually $3) for the visit.

Lynn's coworker Stella belongs to a Preferred Provider Organization, or PPO. When Stella gets sick, she goes to a doctor who has a contract with her insurance company. For most of her appointments, she pays a small fee (usually $10). Stella's doctor is called a primary care physician. If Stella wants to see a specialist such as a physical therapist, she has to go to her doctor first for a recommendation, or else she may have to pay for it herself.

Lynn has an Indemnity Plan. She can go to any doctor she wants, but her insurance company does not cover all the treatments that her doctor recommends. She has to pay at the time of a doctor's visit and then fill out a lot of forms in order to be reimbursed for the payments that she has made.

- Which plan offers health care the most economically?
- Which plan allows patients to choose the most freely?

3 Online

Log onto **http://www.prenhall.com/brown_activities**
The Web: Alternative Health Care
Grammar: What's your grammar IQ?
E-mail: Diets don't work!

4 Wrap Up

When someone has a health problem, decisions have to be made about what to do. The chart below lists some of the health care options available.

Read the chart. Then read the complaints in the scenarios below and make a recommendation for each one.

Lifestyle Factors	Professional Services	Home Remedies and Alternative Medicine
healthy diet	physical examination	ginger or herbal tea
daily exercise	prescriptions	meditation
7–8 hours sleep	visit to a specialist	vitamins
stress reduction exercises	herbalist	herbal medications

"I feel tired all the time, and I can't get my work done."

"I'm sneezing, and I itch all over."

"I can't sleep, and I've lost my appetite."

Strategies for Success

➤ **Describing yourself**
➤ **Using television for listening input**
➤ **Lowering anxiety**

1. With a Learning Partner, talk about a time when you were very sick or had an accident. Then write a paragraph in your journal describing what you just talked about.

2. With a partner or several classmates, find a medical or health-related program or movie on TV and watch it together. Then, together, summarize the program and discuss anything that you did not understand.

3. With a partner, make a list of things you could do to lessen any anxiety you may have about speaking English. Copy that list in your journal and on a brightly colored card/paper and put it where you will see it often.

CHECKPOINT

How much have you learned in this unit? Review the goals for each lesson. What skills can you confidently use now? What skills do you need to practice? List these below.

Skills I've Learned Well

_____

_____

_____

_____

Skills I Need to Practice

_____

_____

_____

_____

Learning Preferences

In this unit, which type of activity did you like the best and the least? Write the number in the box: 1 = best; 2 = next best; 3 = next; 4 = least.

- ❑ Working by myself
- ❑ Working with a partner
- ❑ Working with a group
- ❑ Working as a whole class

In this unit, which exercises helped you to learn to:

listen more effectively?	Exercise _____	read more easily?	Exercise _____
speak more fluently?	Exercise _____	write more clearly?	Exercise _____

Which exercise did you like the most? _____   Why? _____

Which exercise did you like the least? _____   Why? _____

VOCABULARY

Health Nouns
antibiotic
appetite
blood pressure
caffeine
deductible
dizziness
drowsiness
dosage
fatigue
health care
height
insomnia
infection
insurance
irritability
overdose
recommendation
side effects
specialist
stress
surgery

Connectors
after
because
before
when

Adjectives
brisk
soothing
stimulating
unkempt

Talking about Health
come back
get better
go away
pull through
run down
run a fever
Take care of yourself.
take a turn for the worse
under the weather
You'll recover.

▶ GRAMMAR SUMMARY

Complex Sentences with Time Clauses

When I got home, I fell into bed.	I fell into bed **when** I got home.
After I was there for an hour, I became sick.	I became sick **after** I was there for an hour.
Before I got sick, I went home.	I went home **before** I got sick.

Cause/Effect

Because I got sick, I missed my classes.	I missed my classes **because** I got sick.

Direct Speech

The receptionist asked, **"How can I help you?"** Lynn said, **"My friend needs to see a doctor right away."**

Comparisons

Exercise is **as** stimulating **as** a cup of coffee. Getting a good night's sleep is **not as** important **as** studying before a test.

▶ COMMUNICATION SUMMARY

Describing a sequence of events in the past

Before I went to bed, I had to take some aspirin.

After he finished the surgery, he made his morning rounds.

Asking for and giving reasons

Why did you open your mouth?

Because the doctor wanted to look at my throat.

Discussing the relationship between lifestyle and health

Exercise is just as important as a healty diet when you need energy.

Reporting direct speech

The receptionist asked, "How can I help you?"
I said, "I need to see a doctor."

Discussing health insurance and how it works

Under an HMO, when you get sick, you go to a clinic and see one of their doctors.

Under an Indemnity Plan, you can go to any doctor you want.

Lesson 1

In this lesson, you will:

- discuss cross-cultural experiences.
- talk about ongoing experiences.
- make inferences.
- ask for and give an opinion.
- use time expressions.

Reverse Culture Shock

 Read and listen to Yon Mi Lee's letter to her classmates.

September 12, 2000

Dear Friends,

Since I came back to Korea, I've been experiencing "culture shock" again. I remember that I had a similar experience after I arrived in the United States. I felt homesick and lonely, and I was confused. Everybody and everything seemed strange. I've been having similar feelings since I returned to Korea. How can it be? I've been living with my family, speaking my native language, and going to places I used to go to as a child, and still I've been feeling like a stranger. I guess I've been experiencing "reverse culture shock."

I've noticed that I've changed in some ways and my father has noticed too. We had an argument about my future. In the past, I would never disagree with my parents, but since I came back, I've been arguing with them about many things. I don't want to disrespect them, but I feel that I should be able to voice my opinions.

In Korea, we've been taught to listen to our parents and the elderly and to follow their advice. In the United States, on the other hand, children are encouraged to be more independent. They sometimes argue with their parents if they don't agree with them. In Korea it's considered rude to do so.

Although it will take me a while to readjust to my own culture, I am glad I lived outside my country for a while because now I understand my culture better.

Love,
Yon Mi

Pair **What is the meaning of "culture shock"? What does "reverse culture shock" mean? Have you ever experienced culture shock? If you have, share your experiences with the class.**

1 I've been trying hard to adjust.

Pair   Mark with an X what Yon Mi clearly states in her letter. Check [✔] the statements you think are true, based on what Yon Mi says.

1. _____   Yon Mi has been having difficulty adjusting to life in her country.

2. _____   Yon Mi has been visiting the places she used to go to when she was a child.

3. _____   In Korea, children live with their parents after they graduate from high school.

4. _____   Yon Mi lives with her parents.

5. _____   In the United States, parents raise their children to be independent.

6. _____   Reverse culture shock happens in someone's native country.

2 Everything is new and exciting.

When someone lives in a new country, he or she goes through different stages of adjustment. The stages may last for different lengths of time. Read the chart below. Then listen to the students as they talk about their cultural experiences in the United States.

Stages	Characteristics
1. **Honeymoon Period**	• Feelings that a dream has come true • Everything is new and exciting.
2. **Culture Shock**	• Tiredness and an inability to concentrate • Change in sleep patterns and eating habits • Homesickness and sadness • Dreaming each night of home • Fear of being unable to succeed
3. **Mental Isolation**	• Feelings of anger against the new culture • Disappointed in oneself and/or the new culture
4. **Initial Adjustment**	• Feeling of hopefulness • Feeling somewhat connected to people in new culture • Feelings of relief and new self-confidence
5. **Acceptance and Integration**	• No longer trying to change the new culture or making constant comparison to one's own culture • Developing strategies for living day to day

Source: From *Living With Strangers in the U.S.A.*, by Carol Archer © 1991. Reprinted with permission of Prentice Hall Regents.

Pair   Write the number of the stage below the students' names. Then discuss your choices with your partner.

Name:	Oscar	Sofia	Ivan	Lynn	Nelson
Stage:					

Group   What do you think a person can do to handle the stages of culture shock?

3 Lynn has been experiencing culture shock.

Lynn **has been feeling** homesick lately. Ivan and Gina **have been making** new friends.	**Has** Lynn **been feeling** homesick lately? **Have** Ivan and Gina **been making** new friends?

Complete the following sentences based on the characters' stories.

1. Lynn _____ culture shock.

2. Sofia _____ in the United States for two months.

3. Ivan and Sofia _____ friends in the United States.

4. Lynn _____ about her family back home.

5. Nelson _____ hard in the past few months.

6. Lately, Oscar _____ bad about his decision to come to the United States.

Pair Take turns asking questions about each character.

4 Lynn has been calling her parents twice a week.

Pair Look at the pictures. On the line, write what each person has been doing to feel less homesick. Use the time phrases to indicate the frequency or length of time.

twice a week

1. <u>Lynn has been calling her parents twice a week.</u>

once in a while

2. _____

since she came to the United States.

once a week

3. _____

4. _____

every now and then

every day

5. _____

6. _____

5 Word Bag: Expressing Positive and Negative Feelings

Use the expressions below to make a statement about each of the following:

- Middle Eastern music
- French movies
- Latin American dancing
- Chinese art
- Russian literature
- Italian food

1. _____ really fascinate(s) me.

2. _____ doesn't/don't make any sense to me.

3. I find _____ interesting.

4. I have mixed feelings about _____.

5. I can't get used to _____.

6. I'm crazy about _____.

Pair   Ask your partner's opinion about three of the items in the list. Begin with "What do you think about . . . ?"

6 Hear it. Say it.

🔊   Listen to the following sentences. Notice that the sentences in Group A have two strong beats, and the sentences in Group B have three strong beats.

Sentence Stress and Rhythm

A.
1. I like this culture.
2. I dislike this culture.
3. I'm crazy about this culture.
4. I'm fascinated by this culture.

B.
1. I'm very confused by this culture.
2. I'm really not used to this culture.
3. I'm really not enjoying this culture.
4. I may never get used to this culture.

Pair   Take turns saying the sentences. Tap your pencil or finger in a regular rhythm with stressed syllables. Say the sentences a little quicker each time.

7 I haven't received a letter from you in a long time.

Pair   Complete Lynn's letter with the appropriate forms of the verbs.

Dear Yon Mi,   September, 2000

I was very happy to receive your letter. I hope you ___have gotten___ over your culture shock.
                                                            (1. get)
We _____ about you a lot lately. Pablo _____ if you _____ to
        (2. talk)   (3. wonder)   (4. adjust)
life in your country yet. Gina and I _____ to write an article on culture shock ever since
                                          (5. plan)
we read your letter. Nelson _____ the book you gave him about life in Korea, but he
                                  (6. read)
_____ it yet. So far, he _____ about half of it. He says he really
   (7. finish)   (8. read)
_____ it. _____ you _____ a date for your wedding yet? Well,
   (9. enjoy)   (10. set)
take care and write soon. Everyone says, "hello."

                                                            Lynn

In this lesson, you will
- state your opinion about information from a survey.
- read for specific information.

It was good to hear from Yon Mi, wasn't it?

🔊 The students are talking with Mr. Robinson in the Student Center. Listen and read their conversation.

Tony: It was good to hear from Yon Mi, wasn't it?

Gina: Yes, but it sounds like she's having a hard time.

Mr. Robinson: She's just readjusting to her own culture. Lynn, didn't you tell me that Yon Mi also had a hard time when she was here?

Lynn: Yes, Yon Mi is very sensitive to what goes on around her.

Gina: Right. She's very sensitive and smart, too.

Sofia: I wonder . . . when I go back home . . . will I think things have changed?

Gina: Interesting question. But I think it's you who will have changed. By the way, did I tell you my cousin Vito, my favorite cousin, is coming to visit me next week?

Mr. Robinson: From Italy?

Gina: No, he's living in the U.S. He was invited to come and start a new business—a restaurant—with another cousin, Ricky. Ricky is older. Vito is going to be the manager.

Mr. Robinson: Where is it located?

Gina: In New York City. Ricky was told that New York was the best place to open a new restaurant. The restaurant was opened last week.

Mr. Robinson: How is he doing?

Gina: Well, the business is doing great. But Vito is experiencing a little culture shock of his own.

Sofia: What do you mean, Gina?

Gina: Well, he comes from a quiet town in the country. He says he always heard that New York was "the city that never sleeps," and now he understands why. The city is noisy and active twenty-four hours a day. Last week, his next-door neighbors had a dancing party with loud music that lasted until 5 A.M. Vito couldn't sleep all night and then he had to be at work at 7:30 the next morning. He was really upset!

Tony: That sounds like fun! I'd love to visit New York!

Class Do you have difficulty with changes? Discuss with the class.

1 What is this Italian dish called?

Pair   Look at the pictures and complete the answers.   Then ask and answer the questions.

Example:

What **is** this Italian dish **called**?
It**'s called** ravioli.

1.   What is the spaghetti sauce made from?
     The spaghetti sauce _____
     from tomatoes.

2.   What is this cake covered with?
     The cake _____ with
     strawberries.

3.   What is this donut filled with?
     It _____ with cream.

4.   Is that drink served in cup or a glass?
     It _____ in a glass.

5.   What day is the restaurant closed?
     The restaurant _____ on
     Monday.

2 Vito was invited to come to New York.

Pair   Look at each picture and discuss what was happening in each one. Then complete each sentence with the correct form of the verb.

1. Vito __was invited__ to New York.
    (invite)

2. The restaurant _____ on July 2.
    (open)

3. Delicious Italian food _____.
    (serve)

4. All of Ricky's friends _____.
    (invite)

5. Vito and Ricky _____ *(photograph)* for the newspaper.

3 Fabulous New Italian Restaurant Opens.

Read the review of Ricardo's, Ricky and Vito's new restaurant.

Restaurant Reviews

This reporter enjoyed a fabulous dinner last night at the grand opening of a new Italian restaurant, **Ricardo's**. The restaurant is owned and run by Ricardo Poggi and his cousin, Vito Poggi. It is located at Broadway and 91st Street. The opening was attended by a huge crowd of relatives and friends of the owners. The guests were treated to an excellent six-course meal.

Everything that I was served last night was a joy to my taste buds. I recommend it highly. Meals are served family style. Bring the relatives. Enjoy!

All entrees are reasonably priced. The restaurant is open for dinner six days. It is closed every Monday.

Class   What did the reviewer think of the new restaurant? Do you have a favorite restaurant? Tell the class about it. Where is it located? What kind of food is served there? Why do you like it?

4 Young People in the United States

Teenagers today feel good about themselves and the future. At least those are the findings of two recent polls. Teenagers were asked about their relationships with their parents, their feelings about their families and the future.

In the recent poll that was conducted by local newspapers, most teens aged 13–17 said that they never drank alcohol or smoked, and that they are happy with their relationships with their parents. Many teenagers said they are influenced in positive ways by their parents. Surprisingly optimistic, most of them also feel they are well prepared for future jobs. They are skilled at working with computers, and they are not frightened by hard work. Today's teenagers worry about the future, but they seem to feel that they can affect the future in positive ways.

Based on information in "The Millennials Speak," *The New York Times Magazine*, May 17, 1998, pp. 64, 66.

Class Do you think young people today have good reasons to be optimistic? Are the young people in your country optimistic? Discuss your views with the class.

5 Young people today are given many responsibilities.

Read the following statements about young people. Check(✔) the appropriate boxes.

		The U. S.	My Country
1.	Young people are given a lot of respect.		
2.	Young people are often asked their opinions.		
3.	Young people are expected to do household chores.		
4.	Most young people are raised to respect adults.		
5.	Young people are well prepared for future jobs.		
6.	Young people are given too much freedom.		
7.	Young people are taught to work hard in school.		

Pair Ask your partner about his or her responses to the statements in the chart. Then share your responses with the rest of the class.

Lesson 3

In this lesson, you will
- express observations about the surroundings and the environment.
- ask for and give a reason.

The Quality of Life

🔊 **Listen and read.**

A suburb is a place of quiet streets, pleasant sidewalks, and neatly-clipped lawns and gardens. With its large sidewalks and many playgrounds and parks, the suburb looks very appealing. The streets are lined with flowers, and people are always out walking their dogs. The suburban setting feels spacious because everyone has a large house with a backyard. Parents seem content to let their children play outside without fear of being hit by a car. The public schools and services are excellent, and crime seems less apparent. Life just feels more restful in a suburb.

In contrast, the beauty of living in a city is the variety of options that are available. If people want a natural environment, they can find it. If they prefer an environment of cultural and recreational opportunities, it's there. There are neighborhoods and housing types to fit just about everyone. And because there's a mix of people with different backgrounds, the city looks very multicultural and vibrant. A person can walk out of his or her house and right into an Austrian coffee shop, an Irish pub, or a Japanese sushi bar. City dwellers feel exhilarated because of the abundance of concentrated live music, entertainment, and art. Life just seems a little more exciting in the city.

Pair Make a list of aspects of the suburban lifestyle and of the urban lifestyle. Which would you prefer to live in? Why?

1 Touch the water.

<u>Pair</u>   Ivan is responding to Lynn's observations about life in the country. Lynn prefers the country, but Ivan really likes the city. Fill in Ivan's remarks using the verbs and adjectives below.

Verbs			Adjectives		
seem	feel	look	calm	cold	sweet
smell	sound	taste	loud	bright	ripe

1. **Lynn:** I really like the country. It's so peaceful.

   Ivan: <u>I don't like it. It seems too calm.</u>
   _____

2. **Lynn:** And the sun is so brilliant.

   Ivan: _____
   _____

3. **Lynn:** Listen to the birds. They're so musical.

   Ivan: _____
   _____

4. **Lynn:** Take a bite of this fruit. It's so fresh.

   Ivan: _____
   _____

5. **Lynn:** Touch the water. It's so cool.

   Ivan: _____
   _____

6. **Lynn:** And the flowers are so fragrant.

   Ivan: _____
   _____

2 Ivan is tasting the food, but the food tastes terrible.

Action	State
Ivan **is tasting** the toast.	The toast **tastes** bad.
He is feeling his forehead.	His forehead feels hot.

Pair   Complete the sentences below with the correct form of the verbs.

1.   Ivan _____ upset today. The
     _____(1. look)_____
day _____ well. He _____
     (2. not/start)   _(3. taste)_
his toast, but it _____ bad. It is
                  (4. taste)
burned.

2.   Natasha _____ into the kitchen.
     _____(5. walk)_____
She says the kitchen _____ terrible.
                     (6. smell)
She _____ the burnt toast.
    (7. smell)

3.   Ivan _____ a meeting at work.
     _____(8. attend)_____
He _____ very well today. He
   (9. not seem)
_____ his forehead. It _____
(10. feel)   _(11. feel)_
hot. He may have a fever.

4.   Ivan _____ to sleep. He
     _____(12. try)_____
_____ a loud noise. What is the scary
(13. hear)
noise that he _____? Ivan
              (14. hear)
_____ the covers over his head.
(15. pull)

3 The food tastes greasy.

Look at the chart below. Check [✔] your likes [+] and dislikes [-]. Give the reasons for your likes
or dislikes using the verbs in the box with appropriate adjectives.

Verbs		
seem	feel	look
smell	sound	taste

	+	-	REASONS
1. fast-food restaurants		✔	The food tastes greasy.
2. rock music			
3. the suburbs			
4. modern art			
5. red roses			
6. (your item)			
7. (your item)			

Pair   Take turns asking your partner about his or her likes and dislikes. Ask why he or she
likes or dislikes the items.

A: Do you like fast-food restaurants?
B: Not really.

A: Why not?
B: Because the food tastes greasy.

4 Online

Log onto **http://www.prenhall.com/brown_activities**
The Web: Culture Shock
Grammar: What's your grammar IQ?
E-mail: What have you been doing with yourself?

5 Wrap Up

Pair Ask your partner the questions in the chart below and check off his or her choices. Then report your partner's choices to the class.

QUESTIONNAIRE					
	City	Country	Suburbs	Your Country	Another Country
1. Where are you living now?					
2. Where have you lived before?					
3. Where do you think you may live in the future?					
4. Which seems like the best environment for you?					

Strategies for Success

➤ **Collaborating on a project**
➤ **Asking for and receiving opinions and reporting results**
➤ **Reviewing your goals**

1. With a partner, plan an oral (not written) survey of people's opinions on some issue (air pollution, water quality, traffic, etc.). Think of questions you will ask, and how you will put them into a format to elicit "yes," "no," or "maybe" answers with comments. Remember, it all has to be in English!

2. Conduct the survey with your classmates and/or, if possible, with other people who know English. Gather the results and then present them to the rest of the class.

3. Look back at the goals you set for yourself in Unit 1 (Strategies exercise #3). Have you reached some of them? Should you change some of them? Should you try harder? Write your thoughts in your journal.

CHECKPOINT

How much have you learned in this unit? Review the goals for each lesson. What skills can you confidently use now? What skills do you need to practice? List these below.

Skills I've Learned Well

_____

_____

_____

_____

Skills I Need to Practice

_____

_____

_____

_____

Learning Preferences

In this unit, which type of activity did you like the best and the least? Write the number in the box: 1 = best; 2 = next best; 3 = next; 4 = least.

❏ Working by myself   ❏ Working with a group

❏ Working with a partner   ❏ Working as a whole class

In this unit, which exercises helped you to learn to:

listen more effectively?   Exercise _____   read more easily?   Exercise _____

speak more fluently?   Exercise _____   write more clearly? Exercise _____

Which exercise did you like the most? _____   Why? _____

Which exercise did you like the least? _____   Why? _____

VOCABULARY

Nouns	Adjectives	Expressing Positive Feelings	State Verbs	
acceptance	bright	. . . really fascinate(s) me.	feel	smell
adjustment	calm	I find . . . interesting.	look	sound
comparison	disappointed	I'm crazy about . . .	seem	taste
culture shock	fast-food			
difficulty	fragrant	**Expressing Negative Feelings**		
honeymoon	homesick	I have mixed feelings about . . .		
hopefulness	modern	I can't get used to . . .		
inability	native	. . . don't/doesn't make any sense		
integration	scary	to me.		
isolation	sensitive			
relief				
self-confidence				
strategies				
suburbs				
survey				

▶ GRAMMAR SUMMARY

Present Perfect Continuous

Affirmative

I, You, We, They	have ('ve)	been	living here for two years.
He, She, It	has ('s)		

Interrogative

Have	I, you, they	been	living here for two years?
Has	he, she		

Negative

No,	I, you, we, they	haven't	been	living	here for two years.
	he, she	hasn't			

Passive Voice: Affirmative / Interrogative

Passive Voice: Affirmative	Interrogative
The restaurant **is closed** on Mondays.	What **is** the donut **filled** with?
Vito **was invited** to New York	When **was** the restaurant **opened**?

Sense/Perception Verb + Adjective

It's so cool.	The food **tastes greasy**.
And the flowers are so fragrant.	It **seems** too **calm**.

Present Continuous vs. Simple Present

Action	State
Ivan **is tasting** the toast.	The toast **tastes** bad.
Natasha **is smelling** the burnt toast.	The burnt toast **smells** terrible.

▶ COMMUNICATION SUMMARY

Discussing cross-cultural experiences
In the United States, on the other hand, children are encouraged to be independent.

Talking about ongoing experiences
I've been experiencing "culture shock" again.

Making inferences
Reverse culture shock happens in someone's native country.

Using time expressions
Lynn has been calling her parents twice a week.

Expressing observations about the surroundings and the environment
The water looks clean.
The air feels warm.

Asking for and giving a reason
Why don't you like fast-food restaurants?
Because the food tastes greasy.

Lesson 1

In this lesson, you will
- discuss relationships and marriage.
- express agreement and express disagreement.
- give reasons.
- describe emotions.

They think she's too young.

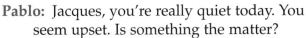 **Listen and read the conversation.**

Pablo: Jacques, you're really quiet today. You seem upset. Is something the matter?

Jacques: Kind of. I miss my girlfriend, Danielle, back in Paris. She's not really my girlfriend, but we have become close friends.

Pablo: It sounds like you're more than friends.

Jacques: Well, we've talked about it, but we decided it wouldn't be a good idea.

Pablo: Why not?

Jacques: Because of her parents. They think she's too young to have a boyfriend. And they don't like me because I'm still a student, not yet established with a secure job.

Pablo: Are you writing to each other?

Jacques: Yes, we e-mail all the time. I don't know what to do. I understand her parents' concerns, but I think they're too old-fashioned, because they want us to look at the world the way they do.

Sofia: My parents think a lot like Danielle's parents.

Jacques: I guess a lot of parents do. I understand their concern for their children, but they have to let us grow up.

Pablo: What does Danielle think?

Jacques: She's upset too. She loves me, but she doesn't want to hurt her parents.

Pair   **Why don't Danielle's parents want her to have a serious relationship with Jacques? Do you agree with Jacques or Danielle's parents? Discuss your ideas with your partner.**

1 She understands their feelings.

Danielle **loves** her parents.	I **agree**.
She **understands** their feelings.	I **don't think so**.
She **knows** their concerns.	I **don't know** about that.

Pair Read these opinions aloud. Use the expressions in the right side of the box to express your agreement or disagreement. Then discuss why you agree or disagree.

1. Danielle **loves** Jacques.

2. Danielle's parents **understand** her feelings.

3. Jacques **likes** Danielle's parents.

4. Danielle **appreciates** her parents.

5. Jacques **values** tradition.

6. Danielle **believes** her parents are right.

7. Danielle's parents **prefer** an older man.

8. Danielle **knows** Jacques's family.

2 We understand her problem, but she doesn't want our help.

Pair Read the letter Danielle's mother sent to Danielle's older sister, who is married. Complete it with the correct form of the verbs.

> April 14, 2000
>
> Dear Nicole,
>
> We _____ (1. need) your help. Danielle _____ (2. think) that we're too old to understand her feelings for Jacques, but you know that's not true. It's not that we _____ (3. not/understand), but that we _____ (4. know) more about the world than she does. We _____ (5. be) married a long time, and we _____ (6. be) parents a long time. We know that romantic love is all well and good. But it _____ (7. not/be) the most important ingredient in a happy marriage.
>
> Would you be willing to talk to Danielle for us? I _____ (8. not/ask) you to convince her that we _____ (9. be) right. Just tell her that we _____ (10. love) her and _____ (11. want) her to be happy. I _____ (12. hope) to hear from you soon.
>
> Love,
>
> Mama

Group What is the most important ingredient in a happy marriage? Share your opinions with the group.

3 Romantic male loves the outdoors and horses.

Group Read the following personal ads.

Romantic Male loves the outdoors and horses; values loyalty and devotion; wants a large family.	**Tender, Intelligent Woman** understands and appreciates sensitive men; respects differences of opinion; values long-term commitment.	**Career Woman** is looking for a professional man to spend quality time together. Beaches, mountains, sailing, swimming, hiking— these are my favorite things. If they are yours, let's chat.
Kind-Hearted Middle-Aged Man seeks woman with a heart of gold, for possible relationship and marriage.		

Match up two of the people in the personals. Discuss why you think they would have a good relationship. Then make up a personal ad for someone in your group. Share it with the class.

4 He was shaking because he was nervous.

Pair Look at the nouns below. Write the corresponding adjectives.

Noun	Adjective	Noun	Adjective
anger	angry	happiness	_____
tiredness	_____	nervousness	_____

Complete the sentences under the pictures using the nouns and adjectives from the chart.

1. Danielle was smiling because she was _____.

2. Jacques was even shaking a little because of his _____.

3. She stopped seeing Jacques because of her parents' _____.

4. She fell asleep in class because she was _____.

Lesson 2

In this lesson, you will

- compare dating and marriage customs in different countries.
- express preferences.
- talk about feelings and emotions.

Matchmaking around the World

🎧 **Listen and read the following newspaper article about matchmaking.**

What is the best way to find a husband or a wife? Some people prefer to meet a spouse on their own. For these people, it all starts with meeting someone at work, at school, in a coffee shop, or even in a grocery store. Others would rather find a husband or a wife with the help of another. These people prefer to go to a matchmaker.

In a traditional country, such as Iran, a matchmaker is typically an old woman who knows all the eligible bachelors in the neighborhood. She goes from one house to another trying to find brides for them by talking to the girls' parents. After the matchmaker introduces the couple and their families to each other, the man and the woman are free to accept or reject the match. The man usually goes to the woman's home with his mother, and the couple talk to each other for an hour or two in the presence of their parents. If they like each other, the families meet and arrange the marriage. If the match is successful, the matchmaker is invited to the wedding and is paid a fee.

Matchmaking is a common practice in less traditional societies too. In the United States, some men and women prefer not to spend time and energy searching for a mate on their own. They would rather get help from professional services. Some applicants are willing to pay hundreds of dollars, fill out forms, see videos, and study computer printouts on potential mates.

Others turn to the personal ads in newspapers and magazines. More recently, matchmaking through the Internet has become very popular.

Although traditional and modern forms of matchmaking are basically the same, what happens after the couple meets differs from one country to another. In Iran, for example, a successful match ends in marriage. In the United States, it usually leads to dating, which may or may not end in marriage.

Group What is your opinion about using a matchmaker? Is it the best way to find a husband or wife? Discuss your opinions with your group, then with the class.

1 Matchmaking and Marriage in the United States and Iran

Read the article on page 74 again. Then check (✔) the appropriate box for the United States and Iran. Then check "My Country" for the statements that are also true about your country.

Matchmaking and Marriage Customs	United States	Iran	My Country
1. Matchmaking is done by computer.			
2. The matchmaker is sometimes a relative or a neighbor.			
3. If the matchmaking is successful, the couple gets married.			
4. The matchmaker is usually invited to the wedding.			
5. If the matchmaking is successful, the couple starts dating.			
6. The matchmaker is usually an older woman.			
7. Parents should approve of the spouse.			

Pair Compare your responses. Discuss the differences and similarities in matchmaking and marriage for your country, the United States, and Iran. Share your findings with the class.

2 When it's time for my children to think about getting married . . .

Read the following statements. Which statements are true for you? Check (✔) the appropriate box.

	True for me	Not true for me
1. I'd rather see my child meet a spouse on his or her own than use a matchmaker.		
2. I'd rather see my child marry a well-educated person.		
3. I prefer that my child falls in love before getting married.		
4. I hope that my child marries someone rich.		
5. It's OK if my child puts a personal ad in the paper.		
6. I'd prefer that my child dates before getting married.		
7. I'd prefer to select someone for my child to marry.		
8. I'd prefer to see my child marry someone from a respectable family.		

Group Discuss your preferences.

3 Hear it. Say it.

Listen to the sentences. Then take turns saying them with a partner.

Contractions with *would rather*

1. He'd rather choose his own girlfriend.
2. I'd rather stop dating him.
3. We'd rather use a matchmaker.
4. They'd rather put an ad in the personals.

5. I'd rather not follow your advice.
6. She'd rather not ask his permission.
7. We'd rather not explain our reasons.
8. I'd rather not tell you.

4 She'd prefer to marry an open-minded man.

Pair   Read the following personal ads. Then discuss what each advertiser is looking for in a man or woman. Write a sentence for each advertisement on a separate piece of paper.

> She'd rather not marry a smoker.
> He'd prefer to marry an open-minded woman.

Attractive, professional. Seeking a well-educated, honest man who enjoys intellectual discussions and candle-lit dinners. Prefer dark hair. In his early 30s. Possible long-term relationship.
Linda

I'm interested in an adventurous man. I'm attractive, smart, and fun. Seeking a man who travels, sails, has active lifestyle. Nonsmoker. Positive attitude. Age 26–35.
Susan

Airline pilot, 41. Separated and new in town. Seeking attractive and open-minded female with a sense of humor. Enjoy museums and reading.
Mark

Very easygoing guy. Mid–20s. Sensitive, but not rich. Enjoy going to the beach and dancing. Honest, friendly, and intelligent. You be the same.
Steve

5 I'd rather marry a well-educated woman.

What characteristics are important to you in looking for an ideal husband or wife? Look at the following characteristics. Add two of your own. Check the three most important ones to you. Which ones aren't important at all?

____ well-educated   ____ funny   ____ athletic

____ adventurous   ____ good-looking   ____ honest

____ rich   ____ good family   ____ _____

____ responsible   ____ famous   ____ _____

6 Wedding customs are similar.

🔊 Listen to the description of wedding customs in the United States. Match the description to the correct picture. Number the pictures.

[ ]   [ ]   [ ]

[ ]   [ ]   [ ]

Group   Discuss wedding customs in your country. Are any of them similar to these customs?

7 Word Bag: Falling In and Out of Love

Pair   Read the letter and discuss the expressions in boldface. Which ones refer to the joys of love? Which refer to the sorrows? Complete the sentences below the letter using the expressons in boldface.

> *Dear Vicky,*
>
> *I **fell in love with** your mother the first time I saw her. However, she almost **broke my heart**. She knew I **was crazy about** her, but she **looked right through me**. In fact, I had heard that she **was involved with** someone else. I felt helpless. I **was head-over-heels in love**, and yet I couldn't do anything. Then I heard that she had **had a falling out** with the other boy, and had **broken up with** him. I seized the opportunity to get to know her, and, well, the rest is history. I know that someday you will find the love of your life too.*
>
> *Love,*
> *Your Father*

1.   Vicky's mother _____ another man when she first met her husband.

2.   At first, Vicky's father was _____ in love, but her mother was not.

3.   Later he heard that she and her boyfriend _____.

4.   Then the mother _____ the father, too.

Lesson 3

In this lesson, you will

- express similarities and differences.
- discuss relationships and marriage customs.
- express results.

East meets West.

🎧 **Listen and read the article.**

Hamid and Elaine Tanori, a New Jersey couple, have been married for five years and have two children. Since Hamid is from Egypt and Elaine is from upstate New York, many of their friends on both sides of the world predicted that the marriage wouldn't last, but they were wrong.

Hamid's story: I think I always wanted to marry an American girl. I worked at a hotel when I was a kid, and I loved meeting foreigners. Many times, I brought tourists home to dinner and my mother would cook for them, so I guess she knew that I was interested in other countries.

I met Elaine in a coffee shop in Manhattan, and although we were strangers, we talked for almost an hour. I liked what she said, so I went back to that same place every day until I saw her again. And the more I got to know her, the more I felt that my life was with her.

Elaine's story: I never thought I would marry the boy next door, but I didn't know I was going to marry someone from the other side of the world either. Now it seems logical. I have done a lot of traveling, and I've always wanted to learn from other cultures, so I was open to the possibility of marrying outside my culture. But Hamid and I have a lot of differences. He comes from a traditional family and I don't, but we try to compromise.

Pair   **Do you think that culture should be a consideration in one's choice of a wife or husband?**

78   **UNIT 6**

1 We have many differences, but some similarities.

<u>Pair</u> Complete the sentences with *and, but,* or *so.*

Elaine likes to learn about different cultures, _____(1)_____ Hamid likes to meet people from other countries. Elaine and Hamid have learned to communicate about their differences, _____(2)_____ they are also willing to compromise. Hamid comes from a traditional Egyptian family, _____(3)_____ Elaine did not grow up with strong family traditions. Many people did not expect the marriage of Elaine and Hamid to last, _____(4)_____ Elaine and Hamid are proud of the success of their marriage, _____(5)_____ their differences always give them something to talk about .

2 Your relationship will change over the years.

Read about the three stages of marriage.

Stage one: The honeymoon
Couples are first getting to know each other during this stage. They do not look at the differences, only at the similarities. Often they like the differences; in addition, their romantic excitement leads them to believe they can solve any problems that come up.

Stage two: The settling-in phase
The husband and wife begin to settle into the roles that they expect to have in a marriage. Often each partner is suddenly surprised to find out that the other may have different expectations; furthermore, each partner may have difficulty making changes.

Stage three: The life-pattern phase
Three things can happen as couples try to deal with differences: (1) The couple learns to enjoy the process of learning new ways to live; (2) The couple ignores the problem. They may try to live under the same roof, but they may not be close to each other; (3) They may choose to get separated or divorced because they cannot make the necessary changes.

Source: Roman Dugan, *Intercultural Marriage: Promises and Pitfalls*. Intercultural Press, Inc., 1997.

<u>Class</u> **In what stage of marriage is each of the following speakers?**

1. "When we were first married, my husband used to spend his entire weekend with me. Now, he spends all his free time with his male friends."

2. "I love the way my wife cooks. Every night I get to try something new and different. I don't miss my mother's cooking at all."

3. "My husband and I like to argue; moreover, we joke about it because we know there will always be some new problem to solve. After fifteen years of marriage, I think we understand the process better now, so our arguments are never very serious."

3 Online

Log onto **http://www.prenhall.com/brown_activities**
The Web: Wedding Traditions
Grammar: What's your grammar IQ?
E-mail: I'm so in love!

4 Wrap Up

Read the newspaper story.

Minneapolis Tribune News   *June 13, 1999*   ♥♥♥ *Lifestyles* ♥♥♥

Matchmaking on the Internet

A young American named David Weinlick and his wife, Elizabeth Runze, celebrated their first wedding anniversary today. They were married a year ago today at the Mall of America in Minneapolis, Minnesota, with 2,000 shoppers in attendance.

Weinlick advertised for a bride on the Internet. Then he asked his friends and relatives to select his bride for him, and they did! And so far, this arranged marriage is working out very well indeed. Happy anniversary!

Group   **What do you think of this arranged marriage? Discuss your opinion in your group. Would you advise a friend to find a spouse this way?**

Strategies for Success

➤ **Reading aloud and monitoring errors**
➤ **Describing people and their relationships**
➤ **Using vocabulary in meaningful sentences**

1. With a partner, look at the magazine article at the beginning of Lesson 2. Read the article aloud to each other. Correct each other if you notice mistakes in pronunciation.

2. Look at the list of characteristics of an ideal husband or wife in Lesson 2, Exercise 5. Tell your partner about a couple you know. Which characteristics best describe each person in the couple? Explain why the combination of characteristics makes them a good match or a bad match.

3. Look at the vocabulary list at the end of this unit, and make a sentence for each word. Write the sentences in your journal. Do the same for the rest of the units in this book.

CHECKPOINT

How much have you learned in this unit? Review the goals for each lesson. What skills can you confidently use now? What skills do you need to practice? List these below.

Skills I've Learned Well

_____

_____

_____

_____

Skills I Need to Practice

_____

_____

_____

_____

Learning Preferences

In this unit, which type of activity did you like the best and the least? Write the number in the box: 1 = best; 2 = next best; 3 = next; 4 = least.

☐ Working by myself   ☐ Working with a group
☐ Working with a partner   ☐ Working as a whole class

In this unit, which exercises helped you to learn to:

listen more effectively?   Exercise _____   read more easily?   Exercise _____

speak more fluently?   Exercise _____   write more clearly?   Exercise _____

Which exercise did you like the most? _____   Why? _____

Which exercise did you like the least? _____   Why? _____

VOCABULARY

Nouns
anger
background
boredom
concern
culture
customs
dating
differences
fear
feelings
happiness
honeymoon
marriage
mate

nervousness
objection
similarities
spouse
tiredness
wedding

Adjectives
adventurous
afraid
angry
athletic
bored
good-looking
happy

nervous
open-minded
successful
tired
well-educated

State Verbs
appreciate   think
believe   understand
know   want
like
love
mind
prefer
see

Falling In and Out of Love
to be crazy about
to be head-over-heels in love
to be involved with
to break someone's heart
to break up with
to fall in love with
to have a falling out with
to look right through someone

Action Verbs
clap   date
compromise   shake

GRAMMAR SUMMARY

STATE VERBS	
appreciate	prefer
believe	see
know	think
like	understand
love	want
mind	

ADJECTIVE	NOUN
afraid	fear
angry	anger
bored	boredom
clumsy	clumsiness
happy	happiness
nervous	nervousness

Prepositional phrase – *because of*

She stopped going out with him **because of** her anger.

Complex sentence – *because*

She stopped going out with him **because** she was angry.

I'd rather/I'd prefer

I'**d rather** marry a well-educated man than a rich man. He'**d prefer** to marry an open-minded woman.

Compound sentences

Elaine likes to learn about different cultures,	**and**	Hamid likes to meet people from other countries
Elaine and Hamid have learned to communicate about their differences,	**but**	they are also willing to compromise.
I liked what she said,	**so**	I went back to the same place every day until I saw her again.

COMMUNICATION SUMMARY

Expressing agreement/disagreement
I agree.
I don't think so.

Giving reasons
She fell asleep in class because she was tired.

Comparing dating and marriage customs in different countries
Some people prefer to meet a spouse on their own.
Others would rather find a husband or wife with the help of another.

Expressing preferences
I'd rather not tell you.
I'd prefer to see my child marry a well-educated person.

Talking about feelings and emotions
I fell in love with your mother the first time I saw her.

Expressing results
I liked what she said, so I went back to that same place every day until I saw her again.

Expressing similarities and differences
Elaine likes to learn about different cultures, and Hamid likes to meet people from other countries.

Discussing relationships and marriage
Hamid comes from a traditional Egyptian family, but Elaine did not grow up with strong family traditions.

Lesson 1

In this lesson, you will
- give advice.
- express obligation.
- discuss job searches.
- make suggestions.

All in a Day's Work

Sofia has been looking for a job. She expected her uncle to find her a job at his company. Listen and read her conversation with her aunt, Alice.

Sofia: I really need to find a part-time job, but Uncle Omar doesn't seem to care.

Alice: Why are you saying that?

Sofia: Well, I know that his company is hiring some temporary part-time employees, but he didn't tell me about it.

Alice: If you asked him, he would tell you. Have you asked him?

Sofia: Not really, but he knows I'm looking for a job, doesn't he?

Alice: Yes, he does.

Sofia: Well, he could at least recommend me for the position. He's supposed to help his niece out.

Alice: I'm sure he would recommend you if you applied for the job. By the way, do you remember the requirements for the job you want?

Sofia: I think applicants are supposed to be familiar with the Internet and have experience with several computer programs.

Alice: What about a degree? Are you supposed to have a college degree?

Sofia: I don't recall anything about a degree.

Alice: So you're qualified for that job?

Sofia: I don't know. But I still think Uncle Omar could get me the job if he wanted to.

Alice: Why do you want this job so badly, anyway? Aren't you supposed to go to medical school?

Sofia: Yes, I am.

Alice: If you wanted to major in Business Administration, this part-time job would be a good experience for you. But I think it would be better for you to find a job in the medical field. I'm sure your uncle and I can help you find one.

Pair   Do you know students who work part-time during the school year or in the summer? What kinds of work do they do? Do you think students should work while they are in school?

1 If Sofia wanted to become an accountant, she'd go to business school.

Many students in the United States find part-time jobs related to their future careers. Match the sentences on the left with the workplaces on the right.

If I **got** a part-time job,	I **would** save some money.
If I **decided** to become a doctor,	I**'d volunteer** in a hospital.
If you **wanted** to buy a car,	you**'d need** to borrow some money.
If I **were** you,	I**'d apply** for a scholarship.

1. If Nelson were interested in politics, he'd try to get a part-time job in a _c. government office_ .

    a. symphony

2. If Yumiko planned to study computer science, she would work part time in a _____.

    b. language program

3. If Pablo were going to become a social worker, he would volunteer at a _____.

    c. government office

4. If Lynn wanted to be an English teacher, she'd work as a teaching assistant at a summer _____.

    d. software company

5. If Tony planned to become a musician, he could work part time for the _____.

    e. senior-citizen center

6. If you decided to become an actor, you could probably get a part-time job in a _____.

    f. summer theater

2 If an angry customer yelled at me, I'd try to stay calm.

Pair   **Read the situations below and discuss them with your partner. Decide what you would do if you were in these situations.**

Examples:

If I weren't happy with some of the company's policies, I would talk to my supervisor about them.
If my boss asked me to work on the weekend, I'd do it to keep my job.

1. You're not happy with some of the company's policies.

2. Your boss asks you to work on Saturday, but you've already made plans for the weekend.

3. An angry customer starts yelling at you.

4. You find out that one of your coworkers is stealing supplies from the company.

5. You're working very hard, but your boss thinks one of your coworkers is doing all the work.

6. Your part-time job doesn't leave you any time to study.

7. Your boss asks you for personal favors, such as babysitting his children.

8. You're asked to train a new employee.

3 Sofia is supposed to be at work at 8 o'clock.

Sofia has just started working part time at a hospital. Listen to the conversation between her and Ana, her coworker. Then write A or S on the lines below to indicate who is supposed to do the job.

Daily Responsibilities

1. answer the phone	A
2. wear a white uniform	____
3. enter the patient's information into the computer	____
4. be at work at 8 o'clock	____
5. fill out the forms for the patients	____
6. contact the insurance companies	____
7. make appointments for the patients	____
8. let the nurse know when the patient is ready	____
9. file papers	____
10. check the patients' insurance	____

Class Then tell the class what Ana and Sofia *are* each *supposed to* do.

4 Sofia needs to pay attention to details.

Read the list of skills below. Put a check (✔) next to the skills that Sofia needs to have for her new job at the hospital.

1. ✔ be organized

2. ____ know more than one language

3. ____ work well with others

4. ____ have a driver's license

5. ____ be good at math

6. ____ be patient and friendly

7. ____ know about computers

8. ____ pay attention to details

Group Tell your group which skills Sofia needs to have for her new job. Explain why she doesn't need the skills you didn't check.

5 Hear it. Say it.

Pair Listen to the following sentences and practice pronouncing them.

Contractions with *would*

1. I'd put on my best clothes if I had an interview.

2. She'd smile if she weren't so nervous.

3. We'd do that for you if you asked us.

4. You'd get some good experience if you worked there.

5. If you were a store manager, you'd work on weekends.

6. If you asked your uncle, he'd help you find a job.

7. If Sofia applied for that job, she'd get it.

8. If they moved to a big city, they'd have better job opportunities.

6 Word Bag: Expressing Highs and Lows

Pair Look at the pictures and discuss the meaning of the expressions under the pictures. What should each of these people do?

He got fired.
He**'s feeling down.**

She closed the deal.
She**'s feeling on top of the world.**

The customer is angry.
She **feels stressed out.**

He lost his business.
He's **down in the dumps.**

Pair Tell your partner what you would do in each of the above situations.

Example: If I got fired, I'd look for another job.

Lesson 2

In this lesson, you will
- identify personal skills and abilities.
- name responsibilities for some common occupations.
- listen for specific information.

Nine to Five

Read the Clear Lake Park and Wild Water Kingdom ad.

"The Best Amusement Park in the World!"
(as ranked by *Amusement Today*)

EMPLOYMENT OPPORTUNITIES!!

Look at what our employees are saying:

You say you can't stand working another summer at the mall? Have the summer of a lifetime! Workers needed for adult and children's programs. Enjoy working outdoors and meeting wonderful people. Salary Competitive.

At **Clear Lake Park and Wild Water Kingdom**, we have the right job for you! Every summer more than 3,700 seasonal employees enjoy working and playing at Clear Lake. We have positions for every talent and interest. Imagine earning and saving lots of money!

As an employee you will enjoy:

★ attending a five-night-a-week employee activity program.

★ participating in free picnics, parties, dances, luncheons, and more.

★ having a bonus incentive program that is the best in the amusement industry!

★ getting discounts on games and gift-shop merchandise.

" I loved working at Clear Lake this summer. It was my most enjoyable summer ever! "

– Park Operations Employee

" I really appreciate having extra money for college. I am definitely considering coming back next year. "

– Merchandising Employee

Interested candidates should send a resume and salary history to:
Margaret Henry, Controller
Clear Lake Park and Wild Water Kingdom
1009 Park Road
Clear Lake, TX 77173

Pair Would you like to work at Clear Lake Park and Wild Water Kingdom? Why or why not?

1 Jacques can't stand doing office work.

Why doesn't Jacques like his job? Listen to his conversation with Nelson.

What did you find out about Jacques? Complete each sentence with the *–ing* form of one of the verbs in the box. You may use the verbs more than once.

work	be	write	keep	apply

1. Jacques hates _____ indoors all day.

2. He can't stand _____ reports.

3. He dislikes _____ records.

4. He loves _____ outdoors.

5. He enjoys _____ with children.

6. Jacques is considering _____ for the job in the ad.

2 Do you like working with numbers?

Make one list of job-related activities you like and another list of those you dislike.

Verb + Gerund	Verb + Gerund
I can't stand I don't mind **working** with children. I enjoy	I hate I like **helping** older people. I prefer

LIKES	DISLIKES
• _____	• _____
• _____	• _____
• _____	• _____
• _____	• _____

Class   Using the expressions listed above, tell the class what you *like* or *dislike doing*.

3 What type of activities do you prefer doing?

People have preferences for certain types of work environments. Look at the six general areas of vocational interest below. Rank them from (1) to (6); rank the one which best describes you as (1), and the one which least describes you as (6).

Realistic workers like activities that are practical and concrete. They like to work outdoors and with tools and machines, using their physical skills.

Investigative workers enjoy gathering information, discovering new facts and theories, and analyzing data.

Artistic workers like having opportunities for self-expression. They love working in unstructured environments.

Social workers prefer working in groups and sharing responsibilities. They like to inform, help, train, or develop people in some way.

Enterprising workers enjoy leading, or managing others for organizational goals and economic success. They like taking charge.

Conventional workers don't mind paying attention to accuracy and detail. They enjoy working under established rules and guidelines.

Source: Adapted from: *Career Development Manual*, 1977, University of Waterloo (Career Services) and Career Coach, Waterloo, Ontario.

Group What type of worker are you? What type of work do you enjoy doing? Tell the group about the kind of work you enjoy doing.

4 The ideal candidate will enjoy helping guests.

Pair Read the ad for four positions open at Clear Lake Park and Wild Water Kingdom. Which job do you think Jacques is interested in? Which job would you consider applying for? Why?

EXPERIENCED SEASONAL CARPENTER
Must own basic carpentry tools. Looking for someone who doesn't mind working on high structures outdoors and in all kinds of weather. Includes weekends and holidays.

SALES ACCOUNTANT
Looking for a mature self-starter with effective oral and written communication skills to promote and sell a variety of group programs to corporate and school accounts. Previous sales experience required.

AFTERNOON YOUTH PROGRAM DIRECTOR
Responsibilities include directing a daily program of outdoor activities for boys and girls, ages 8–10. Must enjoy working with children and have excellent references.

TICKET TAKERS/GUIDES
Responsibilities include collecting tickets at the Park and distributing Park maps. Experience taking inventory a plus. Must enjoy helping guests in a calm and courteous manner. Excellent opportunity.

5 Tell me about yourself.

Listen to Jacques' interview with Margaret Henry. What things does Jacques like and dislike? What things doesn't he mention?

Applicant Interest Profile

Clear Lake Park and Wild Water Kingdom

Applicant's Name: Jacques Fortier

Address: 431 Lincoln Street, Apt. 4
Riverside, CA

Position: Afternoon Youth Program Director   **Telephone:** (613) 555-8133

Interests:	Likes	Doesn't like	Doesn't mention
Working outdoors	✔		
Working indoors			
Working with adults			
Working with animals			
Writing reports			
Keeping records			
Participating in employee activities			
Working with children			
Hiking			
Camping			
Teaching tennis			
Supervising and teaching swimming			
Meeting people			

Lesson 3

In this lesson, you will
- interpret a bar graph.
- interpret information on a pay stub.
- discuss advantages and disadvantages of jobs.

The Moneymakers

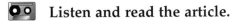 **Listen and read the article.**

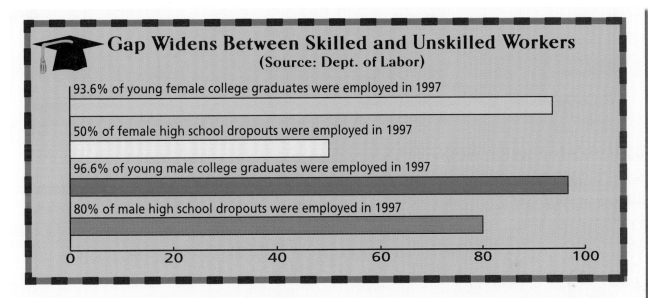

Gap Widens Between Skilled and Unskilled Workers
(Source: Dept. of Labor)

93.6% of young female college graduates were employed in 1997

50% of female high school dropouts were employed in 1997

96.6% of young male college graduates were employed in 1997

80% of male high school dropouts were employed in 1997

0   20   40   60   80   100

For highly educated and skilled workers, life is very good and it's getting better. But the opposite is true for those at the low end of the pay scale. Since the 1970s, the gap in wages between skilled and unskilled workers has widened sharply. But new research shows the inequality does not stop there. Differences in job benefits and the quality of work life have also grown. The need for highly-trained and educated workers is so great that companies cannot keep enough skilled workers on their employment rolls. Consequently, they are adapting to white-collar workers' demands for increases in vacation time, flexible work schedules, and increased benefits.

The good news, however, is that it is not too late for people on the low end of the wage scale to acquire marketable job skills. The argument that education will open a gateway to a better life continues to be supported by statistics. The broadest opportunities, best salaries and benefits, and the greatest security are still linked to advanced education and training. Community colleges and company training programs are currently working very hard to help part-time and full-time students of all ages prepare themselves to meet the needs of the modern marketplace.

Based on information in "Benefits Dwindle along with Wages for the Unskilled," by Peter Passell, *The New York Times*, June 14, 1998.

Group **How much education do you think a person needs to get a good job?**

1 Are you talking about net pay or gross?

Group Sofia is now working at a local hospital. Look at Sofia's monthly pay stub and discuss the following questions:

- How much does she earn each month?
- How much does she take home?

- What happens to the rest of the money?

EARNINGS	HOURS	AMOUNT	TAXES & DEDUCTIONS	AMOUNT	
Regular monthly pay	86 00	$1,032.00	Social Security Tax	$87.57	
Holiday pay	4 00	48.00	Medicare Tax	15.81	
Sick leave	4 00	48.00	Federal Income Tax	119.88	
			State Tax	41.04	
TOTAL	**94 00**	**$1,128.00**	**TOTAL TAXES:**	**264.30**	
Employee Name: SOFIA MANSOOR			**PRE-TAX DEDUCTIONS**		
Social Security: 964-53-6067			Health Insurance	00.00	
Pay Period: 11/1/00 — 11/30/00			Dental Maintenance	5.07	
			TOTAL PRE-TAX DEDUCTIONS	**5.07**	
			TOTAL NET PAY	**$858.63**	

2 There's too much work.

Pair Read Sofia's letter to her family about her job at the hospital. Complete the sentences with *too* or *very*.

I have made some **very** good friends on the staff.
The environment is not **very** friendly where I work.
I am **too** sick to work today, so I'm going home.
I'm not **too** sick today, so I'm going to work.

The hospital where I work is _____ well-known, and the doctors are
₁

_____ well-qualified. All of them are experts in their fields. However, some of
₂

them never even have a five-minute break all day. They work twelve-hour shifts,

_____ long to be able to think clearly.
₃

There are not enough nurses at the hospital. One of the nurses told me that more and

more women are choosing to enroll in medical school and become doctors these days because

the salary for nurses is _____ low for them to live on. In addition, they often work
₄

double shifts—18 hours a day. That's _____ many hours for anybody. Not many
₅

nurses can stand it for _____ long. The hospital is trying to get the
₆

_____ best nurses to stay by increasing their salaries and vacation time.
₇

3 Take charge of your career.

Read the following list and check (✔) the boxes that are most important to you as a potential employee of a large company.

	Very Important	Important	Not Important
1. Enough vacation time			
2. Flexible hours			
3. Friendly coworkers			
4. Professional atmosphere			
5. Opportunity for advancement			
6. Salary or wage increases			
7. Health and dental benefits			
8. Retirement plan			

Look at the job descriptions below. Rate each job according to what you selected as important and not important in the list above.

There isn't **enough** vacation time.	The hours are flexible **enough.**
You have to work **too** many hours.	The health plan is **very** good.

Homer Computers, Inc.
Systems Analyst
Education: B.A. in computer science + minimum of two years experience.
Hours: Flex-time option allows employees to work full time or negotiate part-time contracts; however, employees must agree to be on call during specified evenings, weekends, and during emergencies.
Benefits: Complete Health and Dental package includes choice of HMO, PPO, or Pay for Service option, including family members.
Pension Plan and optional 401K Retirement Plan.
Vacation: First year, one week; second year, two weeks.
Salary: Starting salary ranges from $40,000-$60,000. Yearly raise based on review.
Opportunities for career advancement available.

Mama's Restaurant Corp.
Assistant Food Service Manager
Education: Restaurant management degree or comparable experience.
Hours: Employee should be prepared to work up to 60 hours a week during certain times of the year, which includes being available evenings, weekends, and holidays if needed.
Benefits: Health-care package includes a co-payment for health care, no dental.
Vacation: negotiable, up to two weeks per year.
Salary: $28,000 starting salary. Opportunities for advancement to manager.

<u>Group</u>   What are the three most important considerations for your group in evaluating a job possibility?

4 Online

Log onto **http://www.prenhall.com/brown_activities**
The Web: Employment Opportunities
Grammar: What's your grammar IQ?
E-mail: My Ideal Job

5 Wrap Up: Write an ad for a part-time job.

Pair Vito, Gina's cousin in New York, has just become the manager of his cousin Ricky's restaurant. He needs to hire an assistant manager to work part time evenings and weekends. With your partner, prepare a classified ad for the position. Then read your ad to the class. Use other students' suggestions to improve the ad.

Strategies for Success

➤ **Role-playing interviews**
➤ **Analyzing yourself**
➤ **Seeking out listening opportunities**

1. Find an English-language newspaper and look for jobs that definitely require knowledge of English. With a partner, pick one or two ads and brainstorm some questions you would ask the employer if you were applying for the job ("How much English do I need to use?" "Are computer skills necessary?" "How many hours a week would I be working?"). Then, role play an interview, with each of you taking turns at being the employer.

2. In your journal, write about what kind of a worker you are, and what you prefer to do. Share and compare your comments with a partner.

3. With a partner or several classmates, watch an English movie or TV program (one without subtitles). Then summarize the show with your partner(s) and clarify any parts you didn't understand.

CHECKPOINT

How much have you learned in this unit? Review the goals for each lesson. What skills can you confidently use now? What skills do you need to practice? List these below.

Skills I've Learned Well

_____

_____

_____

_____

Skills I Need to Practice

_____

_____

_____

_____

Learning Preferences

In this unit, which type of activity did you like the best and the least? Write the number in the box: 1 = best; 2 = next best; 3 = next; 4 = least.

- ☐ Working by myself
- ☐ Working with a partner
- ☐ Working with a group
- ☐ Working as a whole class

In this unit, which exercises helped you to learn to:

listen more effectively?   Exercise _____

speak more fluently?   Exercise _____

read more easily?   Exercise _____

write more clearly?   Exercise _____

Which exercise did you like the most? _____   Why? _____

Which exercise did you like the least? _____   Why? _____

VOCABULARY

Nouns
benefits
details
environment
manager
quality
retirement plan
skills
supplies
wage

Verbs
consider
dislike
enjoy
keep (records)
mind
participate
recommend
seek

stand
train
volunteer
yell

Adjectives
flexible
organized
part-time
skilled
unskilled
white-collar

Expressing Highs and Lows

To feel down
To be down in the dumps
To feel stressed out
To feel on top of the world

► GRAMMAR SUMMARY

Unreal Conditions

Situation	If-Clause	Result Clause
Unreal in the present/future	If Yumiko **planned** to study computer science,	she **would work** part-time in a software company.
	If Lynn **wanted** to be an English teacher,	she **would work** as a teaching assistant.
	If I **weren't** happy with some of the company's policies,	I **would talk** to my supervisor about them.

Be supposed to (questions)

Am	I		
Are	you/we/they	**supposed to**	**have** a college degree?
Is	he/she		

Be supposed to (statements)

I	**am**		
You/We/They	**are**	**not supposed to**	**be** at work at 8 o'clock.
He/She	**is**		

Too/very/enough

There isn't **enough** vacation time.	The hours are flexible **enough**.
You have to work **too** many hours.	The health plan is **very** good.

Verb + Gerund

enjoy don't mind hate	**working**	like love recommend	**managing**

► COMMUNICATION SUMMARY

Giving advice
If I were you, I'd apply for a scholarship.
Expressing obligation
Applicants are supposed to be familiar with the Internet.
Discussing job searches
If you wanted to major in Business Administration, this part-time job would be a good experience for you.
Making suggestions
I think it would be better for you to find a job in the medical field.

Identifying personal skills and abilities
Investigative workers enjoy gathering information, discovering new facts and theories, and analyzing data.
Interpreting a bar graph
Since the 1970s, the gap in wages between skilled and unskilled workers has widened sharply.
Discussing advantages and disadvantages of jobs
There isn't enough vacation time.
The hours are flexible enough.
The health plan is very good.

UNIT 8

Lesson 1

In this lesson, you will
- interpret driving regulations.
- identify traffic signs.
- give advice about road safety.

Pablo Takes the Road Test

🔊 **Pablo is taking a road test for his driver's license. Listen and read the conversation between Pablo and the officer.**

Officer: Wait, wait! Didn't you forget something?

Pablo: What do you mean?

Officer: I mean did you check everything before pulling out of the parking lot?

Pablo: Well, I checked the rear-view mirror, the emergency brake, the . . . . oh, of course, my seat belt. I'll fasten it right now.

Officer: No, you don't. You should pull over first, and then fasten your seat belt.

Pablo: Yes, sir. (*Pablo is about to pull over.*)

Officer: Be careful. There's a car right behind us. Whenever you want to change lanes, you must signal first. Changing lanes without signaling can be very dangerous.

Pablo: Sorry.

Officer: OK. Park over there next to that blue car . . . good. Now buckle up and let's go.

(*Two minutes later. The officer looks upset and irritated.*)

Pablo: What did I do wrong this time?

Officer: You didn't stop behind that school bus. Passing a school bus when its lights are flashing is illegal.

Pablo: I'm sorry. I didn't know I had to stop.

Officer: It's all in the driver's manual if you read it.

Pablo: Uh-oh. There's a police car behind us. I'd better let it pass by.

Officer: No, you'd better stop the car. I think we're in trouble.

Pair Do you think Pablo passed or failed the road test? How do you know?

1 You should slow down before an intersection.

These are some common excuses people have when stopped by a police officer for violating the traffic laws. Match the excuses with the officer's responses.

Driver	Officer
_____ 1. Sorry, officer, I didn't see the speed limit.	a. You should keep enough space between you and the car in front of you.
_____ 2. I thought I could pass the traffic light before it turned red.	b. You're supposed to learn about this country's traffic rules before starting to drive.
_____ 3. I'm not from here. I don't know all the traffic rules.	c. You must always carry your driver's license with you.
_____ 4. The road was slippery and I couldn't stop the car, so I bumped into the other car.	d. You should check your license plates from time to time.
_____ 5. I have a driver's license, but I left it at home.	e. You'd better pay attention to the traffic signs.
_____ 6. I didn't know the license plate was missing.	f. You have to slow down when the light turns yellow.

2 Observe the traffic signs.

Group Look at the traffic signs from the United States and Japan. Are these traffic signs the same as or different from where you live? If they are different, draw the traffic signs used in your country on the board. (You can use a driver's manual if you're not sure what they look like.)

> **Parking** is not permitted here.
> **Driving** fast on a slippery road is dangerous.

| Japan | United States | Japan | United States |

a.   b.

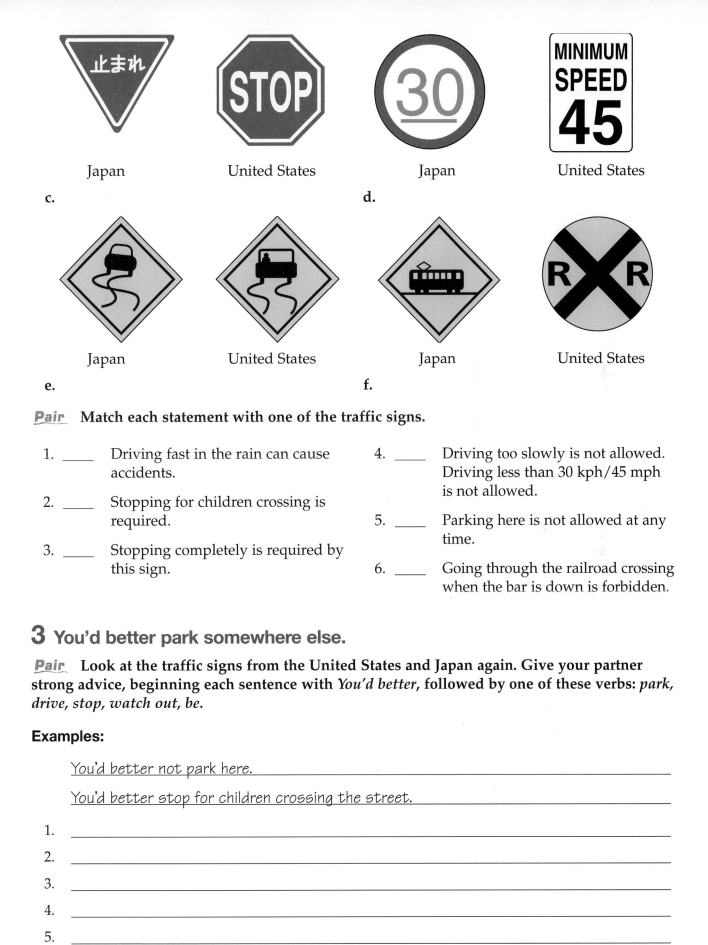

Japan   United States   Japan   United States

c.   d.

Japan   United States   Japan   United States

e.   f.

Pair   **Match each statement with one of the traffic signs.**

1. _____ Driving fast in the rain can cause accidents.

2. _____ Stopping for children crossing is required.

3. _____ Stopping completely is required by this sign.

4. _____ Driving too slowly is not allowed. Driving less than 30 kph/45 mph is not allowed.

5. _____ Parking here is not allowed at any time.

6. _____ Going through the railroad crossing when the bar is down is forbidden.

3 You'd better park somewhere else.

Pair   **Look at the traffic signs from the United States and Japan again. Give your partner strong advice, beginning each sentence with *You'd better*, followed by one of these verbs:** *park, drive, stop, watch out, be.*

Examples:

You'd better not park here.

You'd better stop for children crossing the street.

1. _____

2. _____

3. _____

4. _____

5. _____

4 Getting a driver's license.

Read the regulations for obtaining a driver's license in the United States in the chart below. Then fill in the information about the country you live in or the one you were born in.

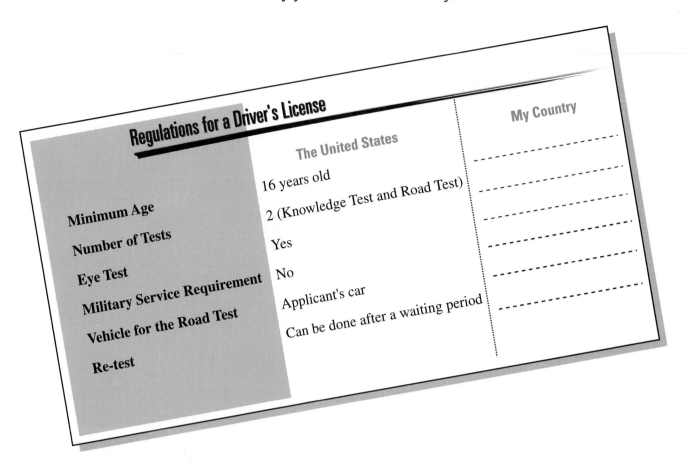

Regulations for a Driver's License	The United States	My Country
Minimum Age	16 years old	
Number of Tests	2 (Knowledge Test and Road Test)	
Eye Test	Yes	
Military Service Requirement	No	
Vehicle for the Road Test	Applicant's car	
Re-test	Can be done after a waiting period	

5 Hear it. Say it.

Pair Listen to these sentence pairs with the same word used as a noun in one sentence and as a verb in the other. Notice how the stress changes. Then take turns reading the pairs of sentences.

Information Focus

1. Last year he had a driver's permit.

2. It permits him to drive.

3. Mr. Robinson gave us a report on our progress.

4. I'm starting to progress in my studies.

5. Did Jacques buy Danielle an expensive present?

6. Ivan had to present his report to the class.

7. Jacques hates to keep records.

8. He records the information.

6 Driving carefully can prevent accidents.

Listen to a police officer talking to the students at the World Language Center about traffic rules. Then, listen again and complete the sentences with the *-ing* form of the verbs in the box. You will need to use some verbs more than once.

talk	talk**ing**	listen	listen**ing**
put on	putt**ing on**	sit	sitt**ing**
drive	driv**ing**	change	chang**ing**
keep	keep**ing**	obey	obey**ing**
be	be**ing**		

I'm Officer Jim West, and I'm here today to talk to you about car accidents. How many of you have a car? Many of you. Nobody likes to be in an accident, so I'm here to tell you how to avoid accidents. _____ carefully
[1]
is the best way to avoid accidents. Most accidents are caused by reckless drivers.

_____ too fast or _____ lanes without signaling can be very
[2]   [3]
dangerous, too. Also, _____ a good distance from the car in front of you
                          [4]
can prevent accidents. _____ a careful driver is especially important
                          [5]
when it's raining and the roads are slippery.

Remember, _____ behind the wheel requires all your attention. Some
              [6]
people do other things when they're driving. For example, _____ on a
                                                              [7]
cellular phone can distract you from driving. _____ to loud music may also
                                                [8]
be hazardous, as you may not hear other cars' horns or an ambulance's siren. There
are other distracting factors too. _____ makeup while driving or
                                      [9]
_____ to someone in the back seat are two examples. Finally, always
[10]
observe the traffic signs. In fact, _____ traffic signs is a law in the
                                      [11]
United States. Any questions?

Lesson 2

In this lesson, you will

- describe an accident to the police.
- call for road assistance.
- fill in information on a form.
- express and accept apologies.
- read and interpret information in a bar graph.

Fender Bender

Read and listen.

Ivan: I'm sorry, officer. I hope you won't give me a ticket for speeding. I was being very careful about driving under the speed limit. It was an accident.

Officer: May I see your proof of insurance?

Ivan: Uh-oh, I think it's at my apartment. I am terrible at remembering these things.

Officer: Do you realize you're breaking the law by driving without insurance?

Ivan: I'm sorry, officer. What a mess!

Officer: Well, you will know next time. You look shaken up. Are you all right?

Man: What about me? What about my van? Aren't you interested in helping the victim here? My girls are late for a soccer game, and I'm on hold with my insurance company. Aren't you going to give this guy a ticket?

Officer: You can make it easier for us all by staying calm, sir.

Ivan: I'm sorry about making you and your daughters late. It really was an accident.

Officer: Mr. Gorki, I have to give you a ticket for causing an accident by following another vehicle too closely, and for driving without insurance.

Man: Now, may I see your driver's license, phone number, and address, Mr. Gorki? My insurance company is going to need the information.

Ivan: *(sighs)* Yes, of course.

Pair How is Ivan feeling? Has something like this ever happened to you? Tell your partner about it.

1 How long do I have to wait for a tow truck?

🔊 Listen to Ivan's conversation with the auto-club dispatcher and fill in the information below.

INTERSTATE AUTO CLUB	Name **Ivan Gorki**		Auto Club ID#
	Location of accident		
	Description of car		
License Plate #		Estimated tow truck arrival time	

Pair   Listen to the tape again. Then role play a similar situation. One of you has had an accident somewhere in your city, and the other is the auto-club dispatcher. Make sure you exchange all the information the tow truck driver will need to locate the car.

2 There are problems with owning a car.

Ivan is tired of taking care of his car. Look at the following pictures and tell his story.

> Ivan caused an accident **by driving** too close to the car in front.
> Ivan apologized **for hitting** the other vehicle.

You missed a payment.

Ivan lost his insurance for _____
_____ .

One way Ivan could solve his problem is by
_____ .

Ivan is considering the possibility of _____
_____ .

Ivan is also thinking about _____
_____ .

Group   How do you think Ivan should solve his problem? Where you live, do you think it is better to own a car or use public transportation?

3 Transportation is expensive.

Ivan is trying to solve his transportation problems. He filled out a worksheet from an auto club magazine. Read his responses and answer the questions below.

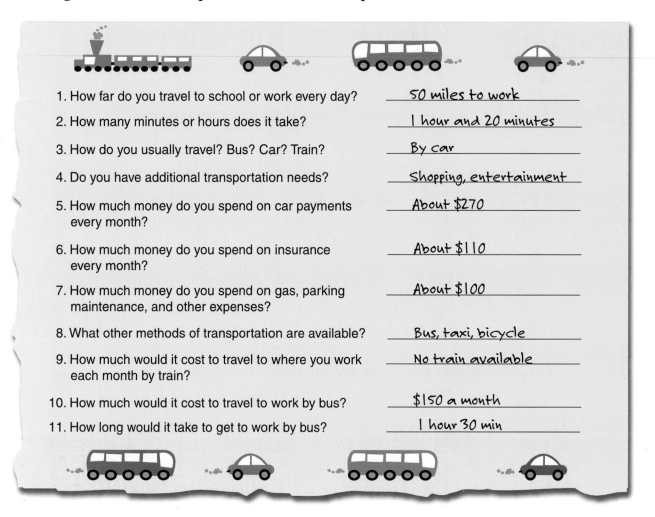

1. How far do you travel to school or work every day?   *50 miles to work*
2. How many minutes or hours does it take?   *1 hour and 20 minutes*
3. How do you usually travel? Bus? Car? Train?   *By car*
4. Do you have additional transportation needs?   *Shopping, entertainment*
5. How much money do you spend on car payments every month?   *About $270*
6. How much money do you spend on insurance every month?   *About $110*
7. How much money do you spend on gas, parking maintenance, and other expenses?   *About $100*
8. What other methods of transportation are available?   *Bus, taxi, bicycle*
9. How much would it cost to travel to where you work each month by train?   *No train available*
10. How much would it cost to travel to work by bus?   *$150 a month*
11. How long would it take to get to work by bus?   *1 hour 30 min*

1. What are the total expenses that Ivan has to pay for his car each month?

2. How much money do you think Ivan would save each month if he took the bus?

3. How much longer does the bus take to get there? Is it worth the extra time?

4. What method of transportation do you prefer to use? Is it the cheapest way to go?

4 How far do you travel to school?

Pair Ask your partner about his or her commute to school or work.

How far do you travel every day?	**How long** does it take to get to work?
How much does it cost per week? Per month? Is there a cheaper way to go?	**How fast** do you drive?

Can you think of any ways to improve your methods of transportation? How could you save time and/or money traveling in your city?

5 Word Bag: Apologies and Regrets

Expressing regret	Accepting apologies
I feel bad about . . .	Don't worry about it.
I'm sorry about. . .	It's no big deal.
I apologize for . . .	Forget about it.

Pair Lynn had a small accident. Match the gestures in the pictures with one or more of the expressions in the box. Then use the expressions to write a conversation to perform for your class.

6 Avoid trouble on the road by staying calm.

"Road Rage" on the Rise, AAA Foundation Reports

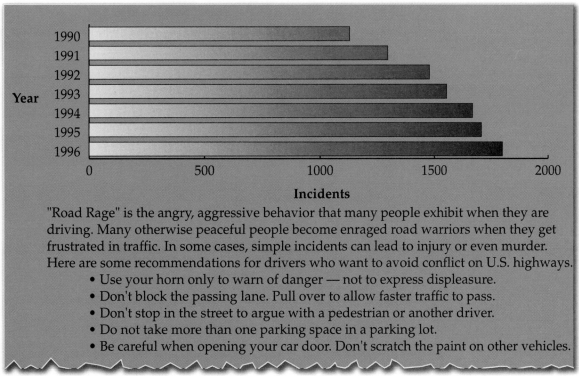

"Road Rage" is the angry, aggressive behavior that many people exhibit when they are driving. Many otherwise peaceful people become enraged road warriors when they get frustrated in traffic. In some cases, simple incidents can lead to injury or even murder. Here are some recommendations for drivers who want to avoid conflict on U.S. highways.
- Use your horn only to warn of danger — not to express displeasure.
- Don't block the passing lane. Pull over to allow faster traffic to pass.
- Don't stop in the street to argue with a pedestrian or another driver.
- Do not take more than one parking space in a parking lot.
- Be careful when opening your car door. Don't scratch the paint on other vehicles.

Source: Based on a report by the AAA Foundation.

Class Why would a driver become aggressive? Has this ever happened to you?

Lesson 3

In this lesson, you will
- give advice.
- give your opinions.
- compare solutions

Teen Driving and Safety on the Road

Listen and read the article.

Sunday, April 15, 2000   *THE LOCAL HERALD*   B-4

Teenage Motor Vehicle Deaths

In every motorized country, teenage driving represents a major hazard. Teens are allowed to get licenses at an early age, and they are not required to have much driver training. Often, none is required. It is not surprising, therefore, to see a higher rate of accidents among younger drivers. The rate is highest between ages 16 and 17.

It is common to see young drivers talking and laughing with their friends in the car, and playing loud music while they are trying to drive. Because they are so distracted, they are not able to handle even small emergencies that come up. These situations often turn into disasters.

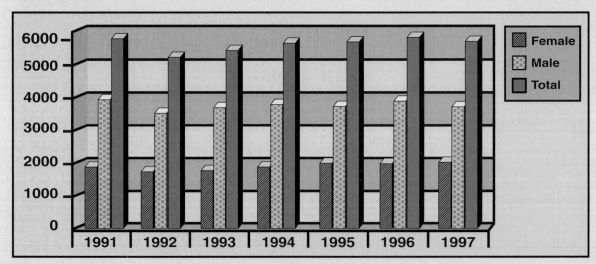

Number of Teen Car Crashes, 1991-1997

Group **What could be done to reduce the crash rate among young drivers? List as many suggestions as you can.**

106 UNIT 8

1 5,697 teenagers died in car crashes in 1997.

Pair Look at the graph and answer these questions.

1. Has the number of teenage motor vehicle deaths changed over the years?

2. Are death rates higher among males or females?

3. Which year had the smallest number of deaths?

4. Did any year on the graph have fewer than 5,000 deaths?

2 It's exciting to drive over 70 miles an hour.

Pair Drivers who are in the 17–20 age group have a one in five chance of being at fault in an accident. Some of the reasons are shown in the illustrations below. Read what the young people are saying.

> **It's exciting *to drive* over 70 miles an hour.**

1.

Girl: It's exciting to drive over 70 miles an hour.

Boy: Yeah, let's go a little faster.

2.

Man: It's very dangerous to go through traffic signs.

Boy: Sorry. I don't have time to stop.

3.

Girl: I love to listen to loud music while I drive!

Another girl: Yeah, it's really cool!

4.

Salesman: It's fantastic to drive the latest-model sports car.

Boy: Man, they're the fastest cars around!

Pair Make up a role-play with your partner. One of you is a young person in one of the scenes above. The other is his or her parent, and is giving the young person some advice.

3 Online

Log onto **http://www.prenhall.com/brown_activities**
The Web: Traffic Safety
Grammar: What's your grammar IQ?
E-mail: It was an interesting ride!

4 Wrap Up

<u>Pair</u>   **Which of these ideas for increasing traffic safety do you agree with?**

Stay alive...

DRIVER ED CLASS

Know How To Drive

NO SPEEDING   Take the Lead...

Cut Out the Speed

_____ lower the speed limit

_____ ticket aggressive drivers

_____ require driver-education courses

_____ take away licenses of drunk drivers

_____ prohibit using cellular phones while driving

_____ require the use of seat belts for all drivers and passengers

_____ increase the age requirement for getting a license

_____ require auto insurance

What are the two most important changes that you agree on? Share your answers with the class.

Strategies for Success

➤ **Reading and reporting on a newspaper article**
➤ **Describing and comparing in writing**
➤ **Setting goals for your own learning**

1. Find an English language newspaper and look for a report of a car accident. Tell a partner about the accident, and listen to your partner's report. Clarify anything you don't understand.

2. In your journal, describe your ideal car: make, model, size, color, cost, features. Tell why you think this car is better for you than some other car.

3. Share with a partner the goals you would like to accomplish in this English class in the last two units. Write them in your journal and make sure you keep reminding yourself of those goals.

CHECKPOINT

How much have you learned in this unit? Review the goals for each lesson. What skills can you confidently use now? What skills do you need to practice? List these below.

Skills I've Learned Well

_____

_____

_____

_____

Skills I Need to Practice

_____

_____

_____

_____

Learning Preferences

In this unit, which type of activity did you like the best and the least? Write the number in the box: 1 = best; 2 = next best; 3 = next; 4 = least.

- ☐ Working by myself
- ☐ Working with a partner
- ☐ Working with a group
- ☐ Working as a whole class

In this unit, which exercises helped you to learn to:

listen more effectively?   Exercise _____   read more easily?   Exercise _____

speak more fluently?   Exercise _____   write more clearly?   Exercise _____

Which exercise did you like the most? _____   Why? _____

Which exercise did you like the least? _____   Why? _____

VOCABULARY

Nouns
crash
fault
lane
license plate
parking lot
railroad crossing
rear-view mirror
seat belt
speed limit
tow truck
traffic light
traffic ticket

Adjectives
cool
illegal
flashing
minimum
missing
slippery

Verbs
allow
apologize
block
buckle up
bump
fasten

fail
pass
pull over
signal
slow down
speed

Expressing Regret
I feel bad about . . .
I'm sorry about . . .
I apologize for . . .

Accepting Apologies
Don't worry about it.
Forget about it.
It's no big deal.

▶ GRAMMAR SUMMARY

Had better

You**'d better** park somewhere else.
You**'d better not** drive fast here. You might have an accident.

Gerund as subject

Parking here is not allowed at any time.

Gerund after preposition

Ivan caused an accident **by driving** too close to the car in front.
Ivan apologized **for hitting** the other vehicle.

Questions with *How*

How far do you travel every day?	**How long** does it take to get to work?
How fast do you drive?	**How much** does it cost per week?

It is + adjective + infinitive

It is exciting to drive over 70 miles an hour.

▶ COMMUNICATION SUMMARY

Interpreting driving regulations
Whenever you want to change lanes, you must signal first.

Identifying traffic signs
Stopping completely is required by this sign.
Parking is not permitted here.

Giving advice about road safety
You'd better not drive fast here.

Describing an accident to the police
I was being very careful about driving under the speed limit. It was an accident.

Calling for road assistance
How long do I have to wait for a tow truck?

Expressing and accepting apologies
I apologize for the damage.
Forget about it.

Giving your opinions
It's fantastic to drive the latest model sports car.

Lesson 1

In this lesson, you will
- describe problems and their solutions.
- make suggestions.
- calculate percentages.
- fill in missing information on a billing statement.

Trying to Keep a Budget

Listen and read the conversation.

Lynn: I seem to spend every penny I make at the photo lab. How can I save some money?

Yumiko: Try to keep a budget. It's like a diet. But instead of counting calories, you count pennies.

Lynn: How do I begin?

Yumiko: Well, first of all, you have to figure out how much money you make.

Lynn: That's easy enough!

Yumiko: Then, you need to determine your expenses.

Lynn: Oh, I get it. If I total my monthly expenses and subtract that amount from my monthly income, I can see how much money I have left. If I get a negative number, then I must be spending more than I make. If I have some money left over, that's the money I can plan to save.

Yumiko: That's it.

Lynn: So if I want to open a savings account and have some money in it, I should find some ways to cut down on my expenses.

Yumiko: Yes. For example, if you decide to take the leftovers from dinner to eat for lunch the next day, just once a week, you can expect to save over $250 a year.

Lynn: No kidding!

Pair Do you keep a budget of your income and expenses? If you do, does this method of keeping track of your money help you to save? If not, do you think you'd like to start keeping one?

1 How much do you spend on transportation?

Pair Look at Lynn's expenses for the month and determine what percentage of her monthly income she spends on each item. Write the percentage in the correct column.

Lynn's Monthly Income: $800

Item	Lynn's Expense	Percentage	Your Expenses	Percentage
car insurance	$50.00	6%		
life insurance	$20.00			
clothing	$70.00			
utilities	$100.00			
entertainment	$50.00			
rent	$250.00			
food	$200.00			
transportation	$60.00			

Then under "Your Expenses," write the amount of money you spend for each item. Calculate the percentage of your monthly income you spend on each item and record it in the next column. Report your findings to the class.

Class Discuss what you and Lynn can do to reduce expenses.

2 Hear it. Say it.

Listen to the following sentences. Then practice saying them with your partner.

Stress and Intonation

1. If you want to save money, you have to budget it.

2. If you eat leftovers for lunch, you can save a lot of money each year.

3. If you want to balance your budget, you should try a budget plan.

4. If you buy only what's on your grocery list, you won't overspend.

5. If you compare gasoline prices, you can save ten to fifteen cents a gallon.

3 If you want to save money, you should keep a budget.

Pair Look at the Tips of the Week and discuss how you can save money.

Example:

If you go to the matinees, you can save money on movies.

If you	**follow** my advice,	you	**could** save a lot of money.
If you	**eat** leftovers for lunch,	you	**can** save over $250 a year.
If you	**want** to save money,	you	**should** keep a budget.

WEEK OF AUGUST 8

When you're grocery shopping, only buy what's on your list and nothing more. Going to the store for a half-gallon of milk is fine, just make sure you only buy the milk.

WEEK OF AUGUST 15

After you eat dinner, make sure you save the leftovers and eat them for lunch the next day. Eating leftovers for lunch just once a week can save you over $250 a year.

Do you know of any other ways you can save money? Discuss them with your partner, and then share your discussion with the class.

4 You have to pay the late payment charge.

Listen to Lynn and a customer service representative talk about Lynn's credit card billing statement. Fill in the missing information.

SaFE CaRD

SAFE CARD
P.O. Box 555
COLUMBUS, OH 43216
Lynn Wang

Account Number: _____
Billing date: _____

Riverside, CA _____
A late payment charge of _____ % will apply after June 5.

ACCOUNT SUMMARY

Previous balance	$ _____
Payments & credits	$ __44.10__
Purchases	$ _____
Finance Charge	$ __7.35__
NEW BALANCE	$ _____

Group Look at Lynn's credit card billing statement again. How much will she owe if she doesn't pay the bill by the due date?

5 Lynn wants to save money.

__Pair__ **Complete the following paragraph with the correct form of the verbs.**

| Lynn wanted **to save** money. | She needed **to develop** a spending plan. |

Lynn wanted _____to save_____ some money, so she needed _____ a
(1. save)   (2. develop)
sensible spending plan. Yumiko offered _____ her. First, they decided
                                       (3. help)
_____ track of Lynn's spending for a few months. They planned
(4. keep)
_____ her cash flow with a personal-finance software program.
(5. chart)
Then they decided _____ some spending traps. They found that Lynn
                  (6. identify)
seems _____ too much money on designer clothes and expensive gifts. She
      (7. spend)
decided _____ to spend less.
        (8. try)
Next, they want _____ some short- and long-term goals. Lynn plans
                (9. set)
_____ a payroll deduction savings account. She'll have money deducted from
(10. open)
her wages and directly deposited into a savings account every month.

After you check your answers, go back to the reading and find the infinitive that follows each of the verbs listed below.

Verb	Infinitive	Verb	Infinitive
1. want	_to save_	6. decide	_____
2. need	_____	7. seem	_____
3. offer	_____	8. decide	_____
4. decide	_____	9. want	_____
5. plan	_____	10. plan	_____

__Group__ **How many members of the group keep a budget? Is it a good idea to do so? Discuss as a group.**

Lesson 2

In this lesson, you will
- offer solutions and suggestions.
- draw conclusions.
- describe feelings.

Wants vs. Needs

Making Their Time Their Own

The average working person today faces more lifestyle choices than ever before. Print media, radio, television, and now the Internet offer people an overwhelming number of choices. But these choices cost money. Here is how four people say they deal with living in a modern consumer culture.

I want to have interesting experiences while I'm young, so I'm only interested in jobs that allow me to work part of the year. I have a strict budget. I only buy used cars, and I live in a cramped apartment. With the money I save, I can have exciting adventures like biking in Alaska.

— Greg Meyer

For our growing family, a satisfying life has meant taking turns working and raising the kids. While my husband was in school, I did the housework and worked at a boring job. Now, I'm pursuing an advanced degree, and he has taken a less challenging job in order to stay home with the children. We both have fulfilling lives as a result.

— Tracy McGuire

I'm concerned about my daughter, Natalie. She isn't talking yet, but she already recognizes brand names. I don't want her to be influenced by TV commercials, so I've tried to get her interested in other activities. Now she is interested in looking at picture books and taking walks in the park.

— Elizabeth Loudon

Our family budget is carefully controlled. We have meetings before we buy something big. If we want to buy new furniture, for example, we talk about what we might have to give up, such as a trip to Mexico. This way we don't get disappointed in our decisions afterwards.

— Henry Miller

Pair   How well do you think these four people are doing? Are they able to accomplish their goals?

1 Ms. Loudon is disappointed in TV programs.

Greg Meyer is an **interesting** person.	He is **interested** in travel.
Elizabeth Loudon thinks TV is **disappointing**.	She is **disappointed** in the choice of programs.

Fill in each blank with the –*ing* or –*ed* form of the adjectives below.

satisfying ➔ satisfied (by/with)   boring ➔ bored (by/with)
exciting ➔ excited (by/about)   challenging ➔ challenged (by)

1. Mrs. McGuire had a _____ job. She was totally _____ by it.

2. Greg Meyer is very _____ about the trip he's planning for the summer. He loves _____ adventures.

3. I feel very _____ by my studies this year. They are extremely _____ to me.

4. Henry Miller seems to have a _____ life. He sounds very _____ with his family and how they make family decisions.

2 I'm stimulated by challenges.

I **am stimulated** by challenges at work.	I **feel annoyed** when I have to work overtime.

Pair **Do you value time or money? Circle the word that best describes how you would feel in the following situations. Then explain your answers to a partner.**

1. Your company assigns you to a special project. It has many challenges, and you will have to work overtime, but you will also make more money. You are

     a. excited   b. annoyed   c. depressed

2. Your husband or wife has been staying late at work. You find out that he or she has been earning extra money to buy you a gift. You are

     a. pleased   b. surprised   c. displeased

3. Your boss calls you into his office for a meeting. He then offers you an opportunity to reduce your hours at work. You are

     a. interested   b. disappointed   c. frightened

4. Your supervisor asks you to work overtime tonight. You will have to give up plans with friends. You are

     a. pleased   b. annoyed   c. disappointed

3 Success means having an exciting job.

Pair Use the words in the box to complete the sentences about success.

boring	relaxing	exhausting
growing	satisfying	fascinating

Success means having an **exciting** job.

1. Success means that you can afford _____ vacations.

2. Success means that you have a _____ career.

3. Success means that you don't have a _____ job.

4. Success means that you have a _____ bank account.

5. Success means that your day is probably _____.

4 He's interested in meeting interesting people.

Pair Look at the following pictures and use the model to describe each person's problem.

Gina is fascinated.	The story is fascinating.

bored/boring

1. _____

depressed/depressing

2. _____

overwhelmed/overwhelming

3. _____

disappointed/disappointing

4. _____

Pair What suggestion do you have for each person? Share your ideas with the class.

5 Word Bag: Names for Workers

When people talk about fellow workers, they often categorize them into certain types. Look at the labels for certain types of workers, and discuss their meaning in context. Do you have similar expressions in your native language?

- A workaholic feels unhappy when he or she is not working.

- A computer nerd is an employee who is totally immersed in computers. He or she often troubleshoots computer problems.

- A go-getter is very ambitious and determined to get ahead.

- A slouch is someone who is lazy and incompetent. Used in the negative: He is no slouch at computer programming.

Match the label with something the person might say.

1. _____	slouch		a.	"I love work. I don't want to do anything else."
2. _____	computer nerd		b.	"I want to be a success and I know how to get there."
3. _____	go-getter		c.	"It takes too much energy to be good at anything."
4. _____	workaholic		d.	"No technology problem is too hard for me."

Pair   Do you know any people who match these descriptions? Choose one of the labels and write a short description of someone you know who matches it. Share your description with a partner.

6 Mr. Robinson intends to take his daughter hiking.

Listen to the conversation from Mr. Robinson's class. Complete the notes about each student. Listen again if you need to. Then compare your answers with your partner's.

Mr. Robinson intends _____ *to take his daughter hiking.* _____ .

Tony would like _____ .

Lynn hopes _____ .

Yumiko wants _____ .

Nelson likes _____ .

Pablo plans _____ .

Jacques wishes _____ .

Sofia wants _____ .

Class   What are your dreams for the future? Share your future goals.

Lesson 3

In this lesson, you will

- read and understand the fine print in ads.
- make polite requests.
- compare products.

The Lure of Advertising

Listen and read the following advertisements.

THE BEST DEAL EVER!

GET 10 CDS FOR JUST $1!   GET 5 MORE FOR $5 EACH.*
NO STRINGS ATTACHED. CANCEL ANYTIME.†
YOU'LL FIND MORE CDS HERE THAN ANYWHERE ELSE.
CALL MUSIC LOVERS NOW!   1-888-555-4535

* plus $2 shipping and handling for each CD.
† You can cancel after you buy 10 more CDs or cassettes at our regular price.

*No pills No diet

before   after

Say good-bye to fat and get your swimsuit ready!

We're looking for 30 people to lose 30 pounds in 30 days.*

*No pills, no diet. Amazing results, FAST.

Call Today: 1-800-FAT-GONE

*Actual results may vary.

Get mobilized. **Get** the **Antenna**.
Make more phone calls. Pay less money.

Call anybody, anytime, anywhere
for $22 a month!*
Get a free cellular phone with
lots of features.†

*Effective for the first 6 months.   †A one-year contract is required.

SALE SALE SALE **Ultimate Furniture**

The biggest sale of the year is this weekend.
More furniture for your money.
No interest, no payment for one full year.*
You'll never want to leave your house again.

*Some restrictions apply. Ask store for details.

Group Look at the fine print at the bottom of the ads. Why do you think advertisers use fine print? Give examples from the advertisements.

UNIT 9 119

1 At our bank, we treat people with more respect.

Advertisements usually have slogans. Read the following slogans and fill in the blanks with *more* **or** *less*.

1. At our bank, we treat people with _____ respect.

2. Your kids will have _____ fun than they can imagine in PlayLand.

3. Fountain Ice-cream. _____ fat, _____ flavor.

4. The car that brings you _____ friends!

5. Auto Experts. Spend _____ money, get _____ service.

Pair **Write a slogan that you've heard or read. Use** *more* **or** *less*.

2 We save you more money.

Pair **Study the following ads and compare the products they advertise.**

Focus Bank offers **more** free checks **than** Harris Bank.

Compare ads 1 and 2.

1. _____ Focus Bank offers more free checks than Harris Bank. _____ .

2. _____ .

3. _____ .

3.

SmartCellular

You talk too much? Good! With 200 minutes for $20* a month, who wouldn't? Save 20% off your calls outside the state.†

Two free cellular phones. Call 555-3987.

*Certain restrictions apply. $35 activation fee required. One-year service commitment required.

† Good on calls made on weekends. Call for details.

4.

save 25% **Antenna** save 25%

Now you can call your mother every day. With Antenna you pay $20 a month for 150 minutes.* You also save 25%† on long distance calls. Did I tell you about the free cellular phone?

Call 2-Antenna.

FREE!!

* $30 activation fee. One-year contract required.
† 25% discount good on Sundays only.

Compare ads 3 and 4.

1. _____.

2. _____.

3. _____.

3 Could you get me a different size?

Make a polite request for each situation. Use one of the expressions in the box.

> Can you help me? I want to . . .
> Pardon me, I need to . . . .
> Would it be possible to . . . ?

1. You are returning a shirt.

2. You need to talk to the manager of the store.

3. You need to use the phone at the store to ask your mother about her shoe size.

4. You just bought a sweater and you want it mailed to your friend's address.

5. You want the salesperson to hold the shoes you just bought until you go home and get your wallet or purse.

6. You want to try on a shirt, but the door to the fitting room is locked.

Pair Choose one of the problems above and role play a situation in a department store.

4 Online

Log onto **http://www.prenhall.com/brown_activities**
The Web: Creating Your Own Ad
Grammar: What's your grammar IQ?
E-mail: Saving for Something Special

5 Wrap Up

Group   **Write a television ad for one of the following products. Role play the ad for the class.**

1.   An ad for a new laundry detergent.

2.   An ad for a watch that is also a small radio.

3.   An ad for a new diet to lose weight.

4.   An ad for a children's product of your choice.

5.   An ad to encourage smokers to quit smoking.

Strategies for Success

➤ **Reading and discussing authentic material**
➤ **Analyzing written material**
➤ **Practicing telephone conversations**

1.   In an English-language newspaper or magazine, find an article, possibly in the financial section, that uses numbers or statistics. With a partner, describe your articles to each other.

2.   In an English-language newspaper or magazine, or on English-language television, pick an advertisement that makes promises to you. Take notes on what it promises. Analyze whether or not you think this product or service will really work. Discuss it with a partner.

3.   Look for a cellular phone advertisement in a newspaper. With a partner, brainstorm some questions you can ask about the product and services. Then, if you are in an English-speaking country, call the company and take notes on the information you receive. If you are not in an English-speaking country, role play such a telephone call with a partner.

CHECKPOINT

How much have you learned in this unit? Review the goals for each lesson. What skills can you confidently use now? What skills do you need to practice? List these below.

Skills I've Learned Well

_____

_____

_____

_____

Skills I Need to Practice

_____

_____

_____

_____

Learning Preferences

In this unit, which type of activity did you like the best and the least? Write the number in the box: 1 = best; 2 = next best; 3 = next; 4 = least.

☐ Working by myself   ☐ Working with a group

☐ Working with a partner   ☐ Working as a whole class

In this unit, which exercises helped you to learn to:

listen more effectively?   Exercise _____   read more easily?   Exercise _____

speak more fluently?   Exercise _____   write more clearly?   Exercise _____

Which exercise did you like the most? _____   Why? _____

Which exercise did you like the least? _____   Why? _____

VOCABULARY

Nouns

balance
billing statement
budget
concern
due date
entertainment
expenses
features
goal
housing
income
leftovers
lifestyle
matinee

savings account
taxes

Workers

computer nerd
go-getter
slouch
workaholic

Adjectives

annoying – annoyed
boring – bored
controlling – controlled
depressing – depressed
disappointing – disappointed
frightening – frightened
overwhelming – overwhelmed
pleasing – pleased
stimulating – stimulated

GRAMMAR SUMMARY

Real Conditionals with Modals

	If clause		Result clause
If you	**follow** my advice, **eat** leftovers for lunch, **want** to save money,	you	**might** save a lot of money. **can** save over $250 a year. **should** follow a budget.

Participial Adjectives

Nelson is **bored**.	The movie is **boring**.
Ivan is **depressed**.	The news is **depressing**.
Sophia is **overwhelmed**.	The work is **overwhelming**.

Verb + Infinitive

Lynn wants **to save** money.	She needs **to develop** a spending plan.

Comparison of Nouns

Focus Bank offers **more** free checks **than** Harris Bank.

Requests with Modals

Could you . . . ?	**Would** you please . . . ?

COMMUNICATION SUMMARY

Describing problems and their solutions
I seem to spend every penny I make.

Making suggestions
Try to keep a budget.
If you eat leftovers for lunch, you can save over $250 a year.

Offering solutions and suggestions
With the money I save, I can have exciting adventures like biking in Alaska.

Describing feelings
I feel annoyed when I have to work overtime.
I am stimulated by challenges at work.

Reading and understanding the fine print in ads.
Actual results may vary.

Comparing products
Focus Bank offers more free checks than Harris Bank.

Making polite requests
Can you help me? I want to return a shirt.

Lesson 1

In this lesson, you will

- discuss recreational activities.
- offer suggestions and advice.
- express enthusiasm.
- express fatigue.

- talk about positive and negative experiences.
- brainstorm possible solutions to a problem.

Having a Good Time

🔊 **Listen and read the conversation.**

Lynn: Wow, what an incredible view. I've never seen such a blue sky.

Yumiko: Yeah, I'm beat, but this hike was worth it. I'm glad you suggested coming here, Jacques. I've never climbed a mountain before.

Jacques: I'm glad you like it. Hiking is my favorite thing to do. Wherever I am, if I have time, I head straight for the mountains.

Yumiko: Really? I guess that makes you a mountain man. To tell you the truth, I'm a beach comber. On weekends, I usually go straight to the beach if the weather is good.

Jacques: The beach is good, too, I guess. I'm crazy about body surfing, but there's something special about the mountains.

Tony: I don't really care where I am if there's something exciting to do.

Lynn: Like what?

Tony: Anything really. I can't sit still. I like to play soccer best, but I also like mountain biking and wind-surfing — anything that gets my blood going. If I can find a thrilling new experience, I'm happy. If I have to sit still, I go crazy.

Lynn: I know what you mean. I love this view, but I get restless if I'm not moving.

Group What do you like to do on vacation?

1 If I have some free time, I go hiking.

Pair What does each person like to do? Look at the pictures and complete the sentences.

| If Jacques **has** free time, he **goes** mountain climbing. | Yumiko **goes** swimming **if** the weather **is** good. |

If the waves are high, _____

_____

If Ivan has the time and the money, _____

_____

If it isn't too hot, _____

_____

_____ if she has an afternoon free.

2 If she's interested in Hollywood, take her to Universal Studios.

Yumiko is expecting a visit from her aunt Aiko. She's calling the tourist bureau. Listen and check (✔) the activities that Yumiko thinks her aunt will enjoy.

| ____ a trip to the beach | ____ sailing | ____ Sea World |
| ____ fishing | ____ San Diego Zoo | ____ Universal Studios in Hollywood |

3 Word Bag: Expressing Enthusiasm and Fatigue

Pair   Discuss the meaning of the following expressions and choose someone in the picture who might say each one. Write the letter of the person on the line provided. You can choose some people more than once.

Expressing Enthusiasm	Expressing Fatigue
1. ____ I'm crazy about skateboarding.	4. ____ I'm beat.
2. ____ Rollerblading® is a blast!	5. ____ We've had enough.
3. ____ She's getting the hang of it.	6. ____ Let's call it a day.

4 Who do you talk to if you have a problem?

Pair   Ask your partner who they talk to in the following situations.

Who do you talk to if you have a problem in class?	If I have a problem in class, I talk to Mr. Robinson.

Who do you talk to if ...

- you have a problem at work?
- you feel happy about something?
- you need to borrow some money?

- you need some advice about your career?
- you want to buy a car?
- you want to take a vacation?

Group   First, one student volunteers to present a problem. Brainstorm solutions to the problem. Then role play the situation for the class.

5 I have a lot of energy when I exercise.

Pair   What activities have a positive impact on you? Use the model to finish the chart below. Then discuss your own experiences.

Positive Impact	Negative Impact
I have a lot of energy when I exercise.	When I don't exercise, I feel tired.
	If I don't get enough sleep, I don't think clearly.
I feel happy in the summer when the light from the sun is strong.	
When I eat healthy foods, I feel great.	
	If I stay home alone too much, I get depressed.

Group   What habits or activities give you energy?

6 You should try mountain climbing.

Group   Choose the person who would make each of the statements below. Write the letter of each person next to what they said. You can choose some people more than once.

1. ____	I love mountain climbing.	6. ____	Be careful! Don't slip!
2. ____	I'm afraid of being in high places.	7. ____	I don't like camping.
3. ____	I just want to enjoy the scenery.	8. ____	You're afraid of heights? Don't try rock climbing.
4. ____	Have you ever gone kayaking?	9. ____	What do you think about white-water rafting?
5. ____	Watch your footing there, Tony.	10. ____	I'd rather go hiking.

Pair   What are three things that you like to do outdoors? Suggest them to your partner. Begin with "I think you should . . . " or "Let's . . ." What new activities did your partner suggest to you?

In this lesson, you will
- talk about vacation plans.
- talk about possibilities.
- talk about past opportunities.
- talk about past abilities.
- give an excuse.

Let's go somewhere romantic.

Tony, Yumiko, and Lynn are discussing vacation plans. Read the ads. Then listen to the conversation.

Tour A

Go somewhere warm.
INDONESIAN HOLIDAY

8 days/7 nights
$1300*
- Relax on the fascinating island of Bali – the Balinese call it the "Morning of the World."
- Visit a Hindu culture with 20,000 temples and 60 religious holidays a year.

Day One: Island tour with a visit to Mt. Agung, home of the gods, and Besakih Mother Temple, the most holy temple on Bali.

Day Two: Denpasar Museum and market – a look at the arts and crafts of the Balinese artists.

Day Three: Free for swimming at Bali's gorgeous beaches.

*Does not include airfare.

Tour B

Go somewhere romantic.
PARIS: CITY OF LIGHT

5 days/4 nights
$995*
- Enjoy six wonderful days of sightseeing in the City of Light.
- Visit one of the world's grandest cities with its numerous old buildings, monuments, gardens, plazas, boulevards, and bridges.

Day One: Morning – Visit Notre Dame and the Louvre.

Afternoon – Have lunch and shop on the Champs Élysées where the rich and famous spend their money.

Day Two: Morning. Visit the Eiffel Tower and the Latin Quarter. Afternoon free.

Day Three: All day trip to Versailles.

*Including airfare.

1 Which trip would be more relaxing?

Pair Read the ads on page 129 again and answer the following questions.

1. Which vacation do you think would be more relaxing?

2. Which trip includes airfare?

3. What are three of the main tourist attractions in Paris?

4. Which vacation would be better for people who want to participate in outdoor sports?

5. Which vacation is better for someone who "wants to get away from it all"?

Pair What do you like to do on vacation? Would you like to visit Bali or Paris? Why?

2 Lynn might want to go to Paris.

Read the statements and make a comment about each one with *may, may not, might,* or *might not.*

Lynn isn't interested in going to the beach.	She may/might want to go to Paris.

1. Yumiko doesn't want to vacation in a cold climate.

2. Tony is not interested in visiting museums this year.

3. Lynn likes the city better than the country.

4. Jacques prefers unspoiled natural beauty.

5. Tony says he wants to try snorkeling.

3 Have you ever been to Hawaii?

🔊 Listen and check the places Yumiko has visited.

Argentina	
Canada	
Mexico	
Indonesia	
Egypt	

Germany	
Kenya	
Brazil	
Turkey	
France	

Pair What countries have you visited? Were you able to speak the language? If not, how did you communicate with the people?

4 They were able to visit the Great Wall.

Pair Talk about places people *were able to visit* on their vacations.

Present	Past	Verb form
can	could	visit the Great Wall.
am able to is able to are able to	was able to were able to	visit the Great Wall.

Example:
A: Where did your parents go on vacation?
B: They went to China.
A: What were they able to see?
B: One thing they were able to see was the Great Wall.

1. Your nephew/Mexico/ the Mayan ruins

2. You and your friends/ Rome/the Coliseum

3. Your neighbors/Thailand/ the Temple of the Emerald Buddha

Where did you go on your last vacation? Tell your partner what you were able to see and do there.

5 I couldn't get a later flight.

Pair Complete the conversations with the excuses below.

I couldn't She wasn't able to	get an earlier/later flight. find a babysitter.

A: I made the reservations for next Friday.

B: I thought you wanted to leave on Thursday.

A: I did, but _____. They were all sold out.

A: Did Alice help you with your packing last night?

B: No, I called Lynn instead.

A: How come?

B: _____.

A: Are you still coming back on Saturday afternoon?

B: No, my plane gets in in the morning around eight.

A: Why so early?

B: _____.

Then make up a similar conversation with your partner and present it to the class.

6 I couldn't hear the music very well.

Pair   Jacques is talking about the first time he flew to the United States. Complete the sentences with *could, couldn't, was/were able to,* or *wasn't/weren't able to*.

My first trip to the United States was very exciting. The flight attendants were very attentive, and I had an interesting conversation with one of them. She said that during the early years of air travel, only men _____ 1 _____ work as flight attendants. Later on, women _____ 2 _____ work as flight attendants, but they still _____ 3 _____ become pilots. Even today, there aren't very many women pilots on commercial flights.

The food on the plane was rather good. We _____ 4 _____ choose French or Italian food. After dinner, I wanted to listen to some music, so I put on the earphones, but there was so much static that I _____ 5 _____ hear the music at all. Since I _____ 6 _____ hear anything over the earphones, I couldn't watch the movie either. I was exhausted anyway, and I _____ 7 _____ stay awake. Apparently, I _____ 8 _____ sleep for a long time because when I woke up I _____ 9 _____ see the Empire State Building. I had finally arrived in the United States.

In this lesson, you will

- understand the content of a speech.
- talk about learning from past experiences.
- write and talk about future plans.
- write and deliver a speech.

But the journey has just started.

🔊 **Read and listen to a graduation speech given by Sofia.**

Good afternoon, teachers, students, and honored guests:

It's an honor to be standing here today and giving the graduation speech. I came here to the World Language Center six months ago to learn English, but I've learned much more in the past few months.

Living in a foreign country with a different language and culture has not been easy for any of us. I remember how frustrating it was at times to make myself understood. For example, two weeks after I got here, on my way home, I stopped at a fast food restaurant to buy a sandwich. After I ordered what I wanted, the clerk asked me, "Here or to go?" It sounds like an easy question, doesn't it? But he said it so fast that I couldn't understand the question. So I repeated my order. He looked at me and said, "I know what you want, but ...," and then he repeated his question. It was really frustrating. There were people standing behind me in line, and everybody was getting impatient, so I left the restaurant without getting anything to eat.

I'd like to thank our teachers for bringing such interesting ideas to class and making our classrooms a great place to develop our language skills. And thank you for your patience and concern for us all.

We are at the end of the semester, but the journey has just started. Some of us plan to stay here at the Center for another semester. Others hope to enter a university, and still some others intend to return home. Wherever you might be, I wish you the best of luck. Thank you.

Group Has learning a new language been a challenge to you? How? Give some specific examples.

1 Living in a foreign country is challenging.

Listen to Sofia's speech again. Circle the appropriate adjectives.

How does Sofia describe . . .

1.	living in a foreign country?	challenging	exciting
2.	trying to make herself understood at the beginning of the semester?	satisfying	frustrating
3.	learning about new ideas?	challenging	fascinating
4.	her teachers?	interesting	demanding

2 Learning a second language has been a great experience.

Pair In her graduation speech, Sofia talks about her experiences at the World Language Center. Describe your own experiences for three of the items listed below.

1. trying to understand spoken English

2. trying to speak English

3. learning about other cultures

4. making new friends at school

5. making plans for the future

3 Hear it. Say it.

Pair Listen and repeat. Then take turns reading the sentences.

–ing

1. Living far from my family is depressing.

2. Learning a second language is challenging.

3. Learning about other cultures is stimulating.

4. Living in the dorm is interesting.

5. Participating in a class project is fulfilling.

6. Working and studying at the same time is demanding.

7. Living in a foreign country is exciting.

4 As soon as I finish my studies, . . .

Each of the students is talking about his or her plans for the future. Read each person's plans. Then combine the two sentences into one sentence, beginning with one of the time expressions given below.

After	As soon as	When	Before

1. **Gina:** First, I'm going to graduate from college.
   Then I plan to travel around the world for a year.

   After I graduate from college, I plan to travel around the world for a year.

2. **Nelson:** I want to finish my studies.
   Then I intend to go back to Mali and find a good job.

   _____.

3. **Tony:** First, I want to learn to write well in English.
   Then I plan to study journalism.

   _____.

4. **Sofia:** First, I have to get accepted into medical school.
   Then I plan to study microbiology.

   _____.

5. **Yumiko:** First, I want to finish my studies.
   Then I'm going to take a semester off and write a novel about my life in the United States.

   _____.

6. **Pablo:** I'm going to complete my studies here next year.
   Then I'll return to Mexico to study aviation.

   _____.

7. **Oscar:** I want to study English for another year.
   Then I plan to become a tour guide in Spain.

   _____.

8. **Lynn:** I'm going to complete my English courses.
   Next, I intend to study photo journalism.

   _____.

9. **Ivan:** I plan to major in English in college.
   I'm going to become an English teacher.

   _____.

Pair   What are your plans for the future? Share your plans with your partner and then report your partner's plans to the class.

5 Online

 Log onto **http://www.prenhall.com/brown_activities**
The Web: Visit a National Park
Grammar: What's your grammar IQ?
E-mail: A Daring Adventure

6 Wrap Up

Pair   **Prepare a speech for the last day of the year at your school. To prepare for the speech, ask yourself the questions below. As you respond, write down some brief notes to look at as you give your speech.**

1. What was the beginning of the school year like for you?

2. What good things do you remember about the year?

3. Can you remember something that is a clear example of your experience of the year? Be sure to tell that story.

4. Who do you want to thank? Write down the names of the people and what you want to say.

Class   **Present your speech to the class.**

Strategies for Success

➤ **Using English in recreational settings**
➤ **Reviewing and analyzing goals you have set**
➤ **Discussing goals with classmates**

1. With several classmates, plan a trip to an amusement park, or a picnic at a beach, or a hike in the country, or a sporting event. Use English the whole time you are together. Try to keep talking the whole time about what you see and hear, what you are thinking, and questions you have.

2. Look back at the goals you set in Unit 1 and reviewed and revised in Unit 5. In your journal, record (a) the ones you completely accomplished, (b) the ones you did not accomplish at all, and (c) the ones you partially accomplished.

3. Now that you are at the end of this course, write in your journal some goals you would like to pursue in the future. (For example, "I will learn ten new English words each week." "I will read English for at least two hours every week." "I will seek opportunities for English conversation once a week.") Copy those goals onto a bright card or piece of paper and pin it somewhere where you will see it every day. Seriously try to accomplish those goals.

CHECKPOINT

How much have you learned in this unit? Review the goals for each lesson. What skills can you confidently use now? What skills do you need to practice? List these below.

Skills I've Learned Well

_____

_____

_____

_____

Skills I Need to Practice

_____

_____

_____

_____

Learning Preferences

In this unit, which type of activity did you like the best and the least? Write the number in the box: 1 = best; 2 = next best; 3 = next; 4 = least.

❑ Working by myself   ❑ Working with a group

❑ Working with a partner   ❑ Working as a whole class

In this unit, which exercises helped you to learn to:

listen more effectively?   Exercise _____   read more easily?   Exercise _____

speak more fluently?   Exercise _____   write more clearly?   Exercise _____

Which exercise did you like the most? _____   Why? _____

Which exercise did you like the least? _____   Why? _____

VOCABULARY

Nouns
kayaking
mountain biking
rock climbing
rollerblading®
sailing
skateboarding
white-water rafting

Participial Adjectives
challenging
demanding
depressing
exciting
fascinating
frustrating
fulfilling
satisfying

Expressing enthusiasm
I'm crazy about skateboarding.
Rollerblading® is a blast!
She's getting the hang of it.

Expressing fatigue
I'm beat.
We've had enough.
Let's call it a day.

► GRAMMAR SUMMARY

Real Conditions in the Present

Conditional clause	Result clause
If Jacques has free time,	he goes mountain climbing.

Result clause	Conditional clause
Yumiko goes swimming	if the weather is good.

Possibility: *may/might*

The weather may/might not be very nice there this time of year.

Suggestion: *may/might*

You may/might want to visit Paris, one of the world's most beautiful cities.

Past ability: *was/were able to/could*

Past	Verb Form
could/couldn't	visit
was able/were able to wasn't/weren't able to	visit

Gerund as Subject

Learning a second language	has been a great experience.

Complex Clauses

Dependent clause	Independent clause
After I graduate from college,	I'm going to travel around the world for a year.

► COMMUNICATION SUMMARY

Discussing recreational activities
Hiking is my favorite thing to do.

Offering suggestions and advice
You should try mountain climbing.

Expressing enthusiasm
I'm crazy about skateboarding.

Expressing fatigue
I'm beat.

Talking about positive and negative experiences
When I don't exercise, I feel tired.

Talking about vacation plans.
I really want to go somewhere warm.

Talking about possibilities
Lynn might want to go to Paris.

Talking about past opportunities
They were able to visit the Great Wall.

Talking about past abilities
She wasn't able to find a babysitter.

Giving an excuse
I couldn't get a later flight.

Talking about learning from past experiences
I remember how frustrating it was at times to make myself understood.

Talking about future plans
I'm going to become an English teacher.